IN THE DECO STYLE

IN THE DECO STYLE

DAN KLEIN · NANCY A. McCLELLAND · MALCOLM HASLAM

GUILD PUBLISHING
LONDON

This edition published 1987 by Book Club Associates
by arrangement with Thames and Hudson

Conceived, designed and produced by Robert Adkinson Limited,
London
Editorial Director: Clare Howell
Editor Lucy: Lucy Trench
Art Director: Christine Simmonds
Designer: Laurence Bradbury
Design Assistant: Sarah Collins
Picture Researcher: Anne-Marie Ehrlich

Colour and black-and-white origination by
La Cromolito, Milan

Printed and bound in Spain

Robert Adkinson Limited would like to thank Margaret Knight of the
Victoria and Albert Museum for her assistance in the following
chapters: American Deco, Mass Production and Deco Revival

CONTENTS

Although Art Deco is a comparatively recent addition to the English language, it is a term that most people will have used to identify a decorative style without thinking too hard. However, unlike the more established Chippendale, Regency or Victorian styles, Art Deco is still ill defined. It has become vaguely associated with the 'Roaring Twenties' and with those aspects of the period which were novel or stylistically daring, and it is understood to convey a mood of gay abandon that completely ousted stuffy Victorian morality—'Take a tuck in that skirt Isabel, it's 1925' (Anita Loos).

Now that Art Deco is so widely used, it would be as well to attempt a definition. The French use the term as naturally as if they had coined it, but it made its first appearance in the English language in the 1960s. Since then it has grown and changed amoeba-like, its meaning varying according to the user and the context. The art historian confines it to the decorative style created by élitist French designers between the wars, allowing it also to describe cheaper imitations of this style. Here it represents the geometric stylization of naturalistic forms, with a degree of abstraction and streamlining thrown in as a natural consequence of this geometric paring down to essentials. It does not include total abstraction or pure geometry—hence it does not include specific schools such as De Stijl and the Bauhaus—unless these qualities are simply used with intent to decorate.

To the radical designers of the Bauhaus the idea of decoration for its own sake was an anathema, and it must have been of concern to them when the French adapted their spartan forms to fit into fashionable decorative schemes with little respect for their philosophical and intellectual basis. But some of the most appealing Art Deco of the thirties did just this and the term Art Deco, by popular definition, has come to mean every aspect of decorative art of the period, encompassing in an eclectic manner luxury, mass production, kitsch, modernism, fashion and the avant-garde. It has come to describe a fashionable style which has no conscience about plagiarism and borrows freely to suit the whim of the consumer. In a word Art Deco is about middle-class consumer style between the wars.

The 1925 'Exposition Internationale des Arts Décoratifs Industriels et Modernes' in Paris was about the art of living in the modern world. In retrospect it was the culmination of a period of intense social and industrial change and, looking to the future, it set the course for the rest of the century. In its fairground atmosphere there was a mood of generous optimism which allowed such extreme opposites as Le Corbusier and Jacques-Emile Ruhlmann to vie for centre stage. Ruhlmann's dazzling display of luxury was undoubtedly the more popular and more in tune with the spirit of the moment, one of euphoria and peacetime prosperity. But Le Corbusier hinted at a philosophy that was more aware of twentieth-century reality, more cognizant of the real implications of social change in Europe, and better able to formulate a design aesthetic for the modern world. This difference of approach reflects the two distinct areas of design during the first half of the twentieth-century: the first centred around the fashion world and up-to-the-minute chic, and the second more concerned with building on the amazing discoveries of the machine age.

The more florid and romantic Art Deco of Ruhlmann and the French interior decorators used rather conventional ideas, merely updating them with streamlining and geometric formality. The flowers, fruit and classical maidens of earlier periods were all used, but had undergone a transformation inspired by Modern Art, in particular Cubism. But the luxurious 'Deco' style of the top French decorator-designers owed just as much to the great traditions of the eighteenth-century cabinet makers. Their aim was to create an atmosphere of unabashed luxury appropriate to the twentieth century and expressing the spirit of the times—or more accurately, one aspect of it, for they were catering mainly for the needs of the new rich, who wanted to continue living in the grand manner of the old rich without any concern for gathering war clouds or impending financial crashes. Many of these clients came from the fashion world dominated in the earlier part of the century by Paul Poiret, who at the height of his career could dictate an entire lifestyle to go with the clothes he designed. This lifestyle centred around extravagant parties, where complete transformation by means of fancy dress and elaborate stage decor created a world of fantasy.

Art Deco was not a movement. It had no founder, no manifesto, and no philosophy. It simply happened because designers and decorators in Paris during the period after the First World War were stimulated by the demands of a re-structured society. Unlike the idealists of the Bauhaus or De Stijl they had no intention of imposing rigorous new lifestyles, but in the process of their work these French designers created a broad new style, which rapidly became popular elsewhere. This style is instantly recognizable because everything was designed to go together and make a complete ensemble; also it is encapsulated so neatly in the period between the wars and the Second World War forced a complete stylistic break in Europe, causing a sharp separation between Art Deco and its successors.

The clearest hallmark of Art Deco is its geometry, which was largely derived from Cubism. Everything from flowers to the human form became angular. Shapes became bolder and simpler as geometry took over. Subjects that were particularly well suited to this treatment featured frequently and have now come to be called the symbols of Art Deco. The sunburst with its clearly defined circle surrounded by radiating lines is one of them; the ziggurat is another, as is the formalized fountain motif with its arc-shapes. Other important aspects of Art Deco were streamlining and jazziness. Speed was considered to be one of the great marvels of the twentieth century—'speed is our God', wrote the Futurist poet Marinetti—and the sleek lines imposed by the laws of aerodynamics became more and more a feature of design. A good example is Lalique's car mascot *Victoire* or *Spirit of the Wind*, a moulded sculpture in tinted glass of a maiden with streaming hair set in a frozen geometric pattern of parallel diagonals. Decorators and designers took particular delight in applying these features of Art Deco to recent technological discoveries or improvements. Light-fittings underwent a complete transformation, becoming sculptural, ingenious or streamlined to complement other ideas within a total scheme. With changing social attitudes rooms that previously were hidden away became a prominent part of the house; kitchens and more particularly bathrooms were 'featured' by designers, for instance Madame Lanvin's elegant bathroom was designed by Albert-Armand Rateau.

The strong simple shapes of Art Deco lent themselves to clear primary colours and sharp colour contrasts. Red, black and silver is a typical colour combination, the red and black providing a background of geometric shapes and the silver acting as a separating highlight or defining ziggurats and other geometric motifs, as in Dunand's metal and lacquer vases. As silver was such a popular colour, much use was made of chrome; glass too was well suited to the bright, somewhat hard-edged look of Deco. Sharp colours like acid green or orange were also popular as they could help to make a shape stand out better. On the whole the colour spectrum of Art Deco is a bright one, saved from garishness by supreme elegance.

Because Art Deco covers such a wide range of design it is difficult to know where the definition ends, for it borrowed freely from what were perhaps more serious design trends like De Stijl and the Bauhaus. Led by Walter Gropius, the Bauhaus architects stripped their buildings bare of ornament and, in an intellectual process not dissimilar to Cubism, were left with a geometric skeleton. Vertical planes, horizontal planes and clearly defined curves became structure and decoration in one, and this basic geometry got stricter as the years went by. As the influence of the Bauhaus became more pronounced the florid geometry of Ruhlmann and Paul Follot gave way to the starker look of Pierre Chareau or Le Corbusier and the Modern Movement. There is a certain amount of overlap between Art Deco and the Modern Movement, but it would be impossible to determine where one ends and the other begins, or whether Eileen Gray and Pierre Chareau fit into one category or the other. In the design world of the twenties and thirties there were extremes of stark geometry, extremes of rococo decoration and countless combinations of the two. But whether the designers said it with flowers or with a ruler and compass, unless they belonged to a particular school, they were all speaking the language of Art Deco.

The century before the Second World War saw perhaps the most radical changes ever to take place in the history of design; it is difficult to imagine anything further apart than the high ornament of Victorian Gothic and the stark simplicity of the Bauhaus, the difference between the Pugin House of Lords' throne and the Mies van der Rohe cantilever chair. Art Deco was the popular, rather than intellectual, response to these changes and in many ways this century is still trying to absorb the full implications of Art Deco; it cannot leave it alone, and has been either re-creating it or building on it ever since it first became established as a style half a century ago. In all its guises Art Deco reflects twentieth-century attitudes, the need for imitative grandeur among the upper-middle classes in France, or the struggle of the German intelligentsia for a new classless society. Just as 'Victorian' is the label applied to nearly all the diverse styles of the nineteenth century, Art Deco is already synonymous with a style that emerged after the turn of the twentieth century and expressed itself most fully during the period between the wars. Every country adapted it to suit its needs, with strikingly different results ranging from Italian Fascist architecture to the Chrysler Building in New York.

In America, where the direct effects of the Second World War were least felt, the style continued without much interruption. Skyscraper architecture evolved with biblical progression, one style 'begetting' the next. The most noticeable effect of wartime isolation was that America managed to evolve a truly American contemporary style. It was based largely on European modernism (chiefly because so many European designers had sought refuge in the States), and was an updated version of Deco. Conversely, the 1950s in Europe was a period when nobody wanted to be reminded of what had just happened and it gave birth to an awkward angularity that will come to be considered as an eccentric by-road of twentieth-century design.

Finally, by the mid-sixties Art Deco was hailed once more, this time like a long lost friend. The great landmark in this Deco revival was the 'World of Art Deco' exhibition at the Minneapolis Institute of Arts in 1971. This took place when the world was just ripe for a bout of nostalgia, and though an art-historical muddle, it was a trend-setting event and established the term Art Deco in the English language. The pastiche Deco jacket for the catalogue became a classic of seventies design and the influence of Deco can be seen throughout the decade, particularly in graphics. The Italian designers especially abandoned the amoeba-like shapes of the fifties for the clean lines of the new-found style that had been interrupted by the war. In the mood of nostalgia that pervaded the late sixties and seventies Deco was a favourite source: twenties sequinned frocks were the most desirable of second-hand clothes; *No, No, Nanette* was staged in New York and London, adhering as closely as possible to the original, and Barbara Hulanicki took over the Derry & Toms building in London to create an updated version of the original department store.

In the eighties the reaction to the so-called International Style of the preceding decades has been the creation of anti-design. In the funky creations of Alchymia and the Memphis group, headed by Ettore Sottsass, Art Deco 'quotes' feature strongly and have become one of the symbols of Post-Modernism. With only a handful of years to go before the end of the century one wonders what else designers can possibly do with Art Deco. Its longevity is truly remarkable.

Dan Klein

1/THE ORIGINS OF DECO

The Art Deco style flourished during the 1920s, the period called by the French 'les Années Folles', and by the English 'the Roaring Twenties'. Another decade in the twentieth century which quickly won a universally accepted sobriquet was the 1960s, 'the Swinging Sixties', a significant feature of which was a full-blown revival of Art Deco. To discover the first burgeoning of the style, however, it is necessary to go back to the decade on the eve of this century, a decade which also acquired its own title, 'the Naughty Nineties'.

Apart from their association with Art Deco, these three decades had in common a flavour of social self-assertion. The authority of conventional morals and accepted good manners was undermined; the established good taste of the time was shaken, never to be quite the same again. The London of the 1890s, after half a century of Queen Victoria's pervasive influence, required the services of a jester who would amuse and shock. The plays of Oscar Wilde were greeted with delight, and the scandals surrounding the dramatist's 'Aesthetic' lifestyle brought a *frisson* to the bourgeois sensibility. The moral sedition which Wilde disseminated was brilliantly visualized by Aubrey Beardsley, 'the Fra Angelico of Satanism' as Roger Fry called him.

Beardsley's black and white drawings were overwhelmingly and sensationally original. They were speedily transmitted in printed form to all the major cities of Europe and America, and their impact was immediate and immense. Not only did they influence much of Art Nouveau, but also, due to the wealth and novelty of their imagery, they were a source of inspiration to artists and designers over the following three decades.

In 1895 Oscar Wilde's homosexuality became public—and much publicized—knowledge, and overnight the Decadents were branded as debauchees. Beardsley's art was no longer merely provocative, it was now evil. So it is not surprising that his followers were few in his own country. But one group of artists, working in Glasgow, had been impressed by his style and originality. Charles Rennie Mackintosh, Margaret Macdonald, Herbert and Frances McNair were involved in the applied arts, and their work may be seen as an attempt to create an environment where Beardsley's figures would not feel out of place, and where Beardsley's ornamental motifs would decorate furniture, metalwork, textiles and posters.

Mackintosh was the architect of the Glasgow School of Art, built during the first decade of the twentieth century. With its large areas of blank surfaces, its tall windows and sparingly used, highly stylized ornament, the building heralded the Deco style. Mackintosh designed furniture, lampshades, carpets, curtains, cutlery and even, in some circumstances, gardens. So his houses and restaurants had a stylistic integrity throughout, which was an important feature of Deco interiors. His work also had the strong rectilinear contours favoured by Deco designers, and decoration was limited to small areas of stylized floral and figurative motifs. At Derngate, a Northampton house he designed in 1916, his decorative style was totally abstract, comprising squares,

Aubrey Beardsley created many of the decorative motifs of Art Deco. Here, in a drawing of around 1895, are the overlapping circles which Ruhlmann, for example, would use some thirty years later; here, too, is the formalized rose which was later used by Paul Iribe and became almost the 'trademark' of Art Deco.

chevrons and other geometrical shapes. Almost a decade before the Paris Exhibition of 1925, he used here a style which would be widely exploited by Deco designers.

The Glasgow group was invited to show furniture at an exhibition organized by the Vienna Secession in 1900. The term 'Secession' was adopted by groups of artists in Vienna and several German cities who broke away from the official institutions of the artistic establishment. During the 1890s the word had much the same connotations as 'alternative' had in the 1960s; it expressed a feeling of revolt, of dissatisfaction with approved taste. Two young architects, founder members of the Vienna Secession, showed a preference for the clean lines and geometrical simplicity which also characterized the work of Mackintosh and his Glasgow colleagues. Joseph Maria Olbrich designed the Secession's exhibition building, an arrangement of cubic shapes surmounted by a sphere of wrought-iron laurel branches, with accents of Beardsleyesque ornament. Josef Hoffmann employed an even severer geometry in many of his designs for furniture and metalwork, but a silver-gilt tea-service designed by him in 1904 has a curvilinear elegance which particularly anticipates Art Deco.

In 1903 the Wiener Werkstätte was established to manufacture and sell the objects designed by the artists of the Vienna Secession. The most important commission undertaken by the Werkstätte before the First World War was the building and furnishing of the Palais Stoclet, the Brussels mansion of a Belgian coal magnate, Adolphe Stoclet. Hoffmann designed not only the house, but also the garden, the furniture, the lighting and the cutlery. For the walls of the dining–room, the Austrian painter Gustav Klimt designed mosaic murals, and most of the other Werkstätte artists and artisans had a hand in the decoration of the house, which was started in 1905 but not finished until 1911.

Hoffmann wrote a magazine article describing the aims of the Werkstätte. 'As long as our cities,' he proclaimed, 'our houses, our rooms, our cupboards, our utensils, our jewellery, as long as our speech and sentiments fail to express in an elegant, beautiful and simple fashion the spirit of our own times, we will continue to be immeasurably far behind our forefathers, and no amount of lies can deceive us about all these weaknesses.' For many avant-garde architects and designers at the turn of the century the 'spirit of our times' was embodied in modern technology and recently introduced materials. Reinforced concrete, plate glass, aluminium, ebonite, linoleum were all used by Otto Wagner (both Olbrich and Hoffmann's mentor) in the Post Office Savings Bank he built for Vienna between 1904 and 1912. In a world of motor cars, telephones, elevators and domestic appliances powered by electricity, the historical styles of architecture and ornament seemed to many designers to be inappropriate and irrelevant.

The need for a style suitable to the modern age was particularly pressing in America, where the art of the past was not only an anachronism but also a geographical anomaly. In 1898 the American architect Russell Sturgis wrote: 'The old styles simply do not apply to us, and we have to disregard them. . . . If the architects were to fall back upon their building, their construction, their handling of materials as their sole source of architectural effect, a new and valuable style might take form.'

During the 1890s a number of Chicago architects designed several large commercial buildings which were almost entirely free of ornament. As the electric elevator was perfected, skyscrapers grew higher and higher. One or two of them were surmounted by a Classical temple or a Gothic spire, but it was soon perceived by the architects that this was a novel form of building, born of technological progress and new materials, and therefore it should be decorated, if at all, in an original style. So early in the twentieth century skyscrapers were bedecked in ornament symbolizing the dynamic of science and commerce, rather than the forces of the natural world which ornament had traditionally represented.

Meanwhile, Frank Lloyd Wright was developing a style of domestic architecture equally devoid of historical reference. Wright, who from an early age had been made aware of the simple, coloured, toy bricks designed by the German educator Friedrich Froebel, built houses composed of geometrical blocks. He furnished them in a plain, geometric style, related to the English Arts and Crafts movement but not at all evocative of any quaint rusticity. Wright's furniture is urbane and stylish, unequivocally modern; other American designers followed the path he had beaten.

In Amsterdam, too, there were pioneering designers whose work clearly announced the simplicity and elegance of Art Deco. H. P. Berlage was a successful architect who, in 1900, opened a shop in Amsterdam called t'Binnenhuis (The House Interior) where it was possible to buy furniture and glassware designed by the architect, as well as pottery, metalwork and textiles by a group of young designers. There was C. J. van der Hoef, who designed pottery for the Amstelhoek factory, decorated with geometric ornament; there was Jan Eissenlöffel, a highly inventive silversmith.

So, even in 1900, the year of the Paris Exhibition and the apotheosis of Art Nouveau, there were, in several places across Europe and the USA, groups of designers working in a quite distinct style. Opposed to the sweeping, irregular curves of Art Nouveau, these designers favoured a simple geometry, and instead of allowing flora and fauna to writhe all over their work, their ornament, if any, was contained, stylized and deliberately flat. Nevertheless, this more formal concept of design had in common with Art Nouveau what is implied in the latter's title. What the artists of the turn of the century were striving to achieve was a style which could not be labelled as a revival—Classical, Gothic, Renaissance, Henri IV, Louis XIV, Tudor, Georgian, Empire, Regency or any of the other styles imitated by nineteenth-century designers seeking to satisfy the contemporary demand for historical sophistication. Art Nouveau was not so much 'new' in the sense of 'different' as 'new' in the sense of 'modern', and to that extent the designers in Glasgow, Vienna, Chicago, Amsterdam and elsewhere, who worked in a geometric style foreshadowing Art Deco, may be classified as Art Nouveau.

The organizers of an international exhibition of the decorative arts held in Turin in 1902 stipulated that none of the exhibits should display any reference to 'previous styles'. Roger Marx, the French critic, writing of another projected exhibition in 1907 stated: 'We want it to be modern so that any reminiscence of the past is ruthlessly excluded.' Many artists employed both the sinuous line of Art Nouveau and the rigid geometry of the more forward-looking style, and those that did usually developed from the former to the latter.

Underlying the vehement urge among so many designers to develop modern solutions to old problems, there was an awareness that the advent of the twentieth century made it essential to abandon nineteenth-century attitudes. Nor was this merely a romantic whim. During the 1890s life in Europe and the USA was rapidly changing. Since the unification of Germany and Italy, Europe had had an extensive railway network; all towns were interconnected by regular trains, and ideas as well as passengers and freight moved faster and further. Advanced theories of biology, physics, sociology, psychology and the arts were rapidly transmitted via telegraph, railways and the new cheap press throughout the civilized world.

One particular development in the technology of communications was of enormous importance to the visual arts—the means of reproducing photographs in mass-circulation newspapers and periodicals. Many art magazines were beautifully printed on handmade paper and illustrated with line drawings and woodcuts, but they were expensive and only distributed among a small circle of enthusiasts. *The Studio,* which was first issued in 1893, was an entirely different sort of magazine. It reported the activities of a wide range of artists, architects and craftsmen, and most of its reports were illustrated with photographs of their work. It was widely distributed: Picasso read it in Barcelona, Hoffmann in Vienna, Wright in Chicago. In some of the places where the pages of *The Studio* were perused, an attempt was made to emulate the periodical locally. From 1895, *Pan* was published in Berlin; in 1897, *Art et Décoration* and *L'Art Décoratif* were started in France, and the same year, in Germany, *Deutsche Kunst und Dekoration* and *Dekorative Kunst* both appeared; the following year *Kunst und Kunsthandwerk* began to be published in Austria, and the Vienna Secession started their own magazine, *Ver Sacrum.* Each new issue of each new magazine, with its photographs of some of the radical developments in the applied arts, was widely disseminated, and each innovation spawned others until there was a mêlée of styles and theories. From it would emerge Art Deco.

Nowhere was the confusion of modern tendencies in design more evident than in Germany at the turn of the century. In Munich, Obrist, Endell and Pankok represented a local version of Art Nouveau based on natural forms, the whiplash line of a wild cyclamen or the fluid shape of a protozoan creature. In Darmstadt, the Grand Duke Ernst-Ludwig of Hesse employed English designers working in the more sober Arts and Crafts style. In Berlin and Weimar, the Belgian architect and designer Henry van de Velde was favoured, with his abstract variant of Art Nouveau. Richard Riemerschmid and Aldebert Niemeyer, both working mainly in Munich, created their own versions of the van de Velde style. At his workshop in Dresden, Karl Schmidt was producing inexpensive furniture by machine in a simple, geometric style.

Whereas in England the Arts and Crafts movement was primarily a middle-class whim and in France Art Nouveau was a passing fashion, in Germany an economic imperative lay beneath the search for a modern style. German industry was fighting for a place in the European market for every kind of household goods. Therefore design was of vital importance, and with Teutonic thoroughness the German government set about searching for the right formula. Hermann Muthesius, a civil servant, was appointed to investigate the matter. After a prolonged visit to Britain, and an exhaustive survey of developments there in architecture and design, he proposed the Glasgow style as the most appropriate for German industry. His choice was supported by developments in Darmstadt, where the Grand Duke had established an artists' colony, Matildenhöhe. The architect chosen to design most of the important buildings was Olbrich, from Vienna, already an admirer of Mackintosh's style. In 1901 a volume of the Glasgow architect's designs for the home of a connoisseur was published in Darmstadt. Peter Behrens, a painter and designer from Munich, was also invited to Matildenhöhe and soon created his own version of the Glasgow style.

Behrens worked closely with Muthesius, and the next tendency to develop in his style concurred with the drift of the latter's theory. Muthesius realized that it was necessary to forge closer links between design and industry. The individualistic expression of a van de Velde was incompatible with efficient production. Muthesius sought to impose on designers a degree of standardization which would be appropriate for manufacture by machinery and which would give German products an identifiable look. He recalled his years in England and his admiration for the uniformity of Georgian terraces, furniture and silverware. A similar uniformity had been achieved in Prussia during the early nineteenth century with the neo-classical architecture of Schinkel, whose buildings were a series of well-proportioned bays with a minimum of ornament. So, when Behrens was appointed designer to the vast electrical company AEG, he worked in a neo-classical style. Almost everything which Behrens designed for AEG, from turbine factories to electric kettles, from office buildings to publicity material, had a Schinkelesque flavour.

In 1907, the same year that Behrens started working for AEG, the Deutscher Werkbund was founded. It was an association of manufacturers, designers and craftsmen and its aim was to create a liaison between industry and design. Through the Werkbund's conferences

Electric kettle designed by Peter Behrens for AEG, around 1908. Behrens applied to all his designs for the giant electrical company a style derived from the neo-classicism of the early nineteenth-century architect K.F. Schinkel.

and year-books Muthesius propagated the ideal of standardization and the neo-classical style. Gradually designers were won over and the idiosyncrasies which had characterized German products for the previous ten years began to vanish.

The style which emerged in Germany during the first decade of the twentieth century was distinctly modern and at the same time had the authority—and the chic—of historical precedent. When the Deutsche Werkbund exhibited some interiors in Paris at the Salon d'Automne of 1910, they were enthusiastically applauded by the French who had not seen a decorative style displayed with such coherence and conviction since the Art Nouveau ensembles of 1900. It was in France over the next fifteen years that the Deco style was to mature, and the German exhibit at the 1910 Salon d'Automne contributed to the final confection.

What had happened in France since the gates closed on the 1900 Exposition Universelle in Paris? The Art Nouveau style which had permeated most of its pavilions was quickly dropped. It was a style which led nowhere, and although refreshingly free of historical references, did not seem to be infused with the spirit of the new century. As a result of Art Nouveau's demise, the decade which followed might have been called *les années des antiquaires*. Almost as if ashamed, through support of Art Nouveau, of having committed an error of bad taste, French householders reacted by buying their furniture from the antique-dealers, favouring the neo-classical styles of Louis XVI and Louis Philippe. Certainly, France did have an equivalent of Mackintosh in Britain or Wright in the USA: Auguste Perret designed a block of flats in the Rue Franklin, Paris, built between 1902 and 1903, which, true to its concrete construction, had a facade rigidly divided into rectangles. Maiolica tiles patterned with flower-heads filled the areas between the constructional members, giving the building a somewhat Deco appearance.

Some Parisian designers who had been practitioners of Art Nouveau abandoned the style and sought new inspiration. Maurice Dufrène, who had worked for La Maison Moderne, one of the leading retailers of Art Nouveau design, vigorously condemned the style's extravagant ornament and turned to a much simpler idiom inspired by French country furniture; the young artist André Mare also designed furniture influenced by provincial styles. Paul Follot, who had also worked for La Maison Moderne, set out to adapt the forms of the late eighteenth century to modern life. The designer Léon Jallot, who until 1903 was the director of the workshops supplying another gallery, La Maison de l'Art Nouveau, reacted in a similar way. René Lalique gradually gave up making the Art Nouveau jewellery which had earned him such fame and riches during the 1890s and turned to the manufacture of glass. In 1908 the parfumier François Coty invited him to design scent-bottles, and although the bottle he created for La Libellule has echoes of his Art Nouveau jewellery, the range of bottles generally prefigures the glass which he was to produce during the 1920s. Lalique also created for Coty a circular cardboard box, for face-powder, covered in a design of

Chair designed by André Mare in cherrywood with a straw seat, exhibited in Paris at the 1911 Salon d'Automne. The chair shows Mare's association with Cubist painters and sculptors, but its style is primarily derived from traditional French country design.

powder-puffs in orange, black, gold and white, an early example of the eye-catching packaging which became prevalent in the years following the First World War.

In 1911 Paul Poiret the couturier started making a range of scents and, noting Coty's success, paid particular attention to the bottles and packaging. Poiret himself modelled the bottles in plaster. The novelty and elegance of these bottles, and the boxes in which the scents were sold, indicated that a new force had appeared in the field of the decorative arts. When the Exposition des Arts Décoratifs of 1925 was being arranged the commissioner general of the exhibition and a representative of the Ministère des Beaux-Arts publicly announced: 'It is only possible to hold this event because of the impetus which Paul Poiret has given to the modern decorative arts . . . .'

Poiret had already revolutionized the world of women's fashion. About 1904 he had introduced a range of clear, bright colours for dress fabrics, reacting against the softer shades favoured by the Art Nouveau designers, which had characterized the years round 1900. He had liberated the female body from the corset and made pantaloons and the turban fashionable. As a keen amateur painter he commissioned promising young artists to work for him. In 1908 he bought a Louis XVI mansion on the Avenue d'Antin which he had remodelled by a designer who was to become one of the masters of Art Deco: Louis Süe. To design his letter-heads, a different one for each day of the week, he commissioned Raoul Dufy, the start of a successful association. To publicize his fashions he issued albums printed from designs by Paul Iribe and Georges Lepape, which, more than any other creation, demonstrate the profound influence of Beardsley on Art Deco.

Then, in 1909, Serge Diaghilev brought the Russian ballet to Paris. It caused a sensation. Not only the brightly coloured, exotic costumes and the lavish scenery, designed by Léon Bakst and Alexandre Benois, but also the vigorous, sensuous movements of the dancers thrilled the audiences, and seemed to endorse the style that Poiret had been promoting. Here, on the stage of the Châtelet theatre, was all the grace, elegance and undisguised sexual allure which the style of Poiret's fashions had promised.

Impressed by the Deutscher Werkbund exhibits at the Salon d'Automne of 1910, Poiret made a point, when visiting Germany and Austria immediately afterwards, of meeting designers and seeing more of their work. He also went to Brussels to stay in the Palais Stoclet, which had become a total expression of the early Wiener Werkstätte style, geometric, elegant, and rich in materials, but a little formal and severe. It had taken over five years to complete and by the time it was finished in 1910 there was a new wave of Werkstätte designers, such as Dagobert Peche and Eduard Wimmer, who were working in a more relaxed style using decorative motifs largely based on Austrian peasant ornament. A group of designers in Prague (then part of the Austro-Hungarian empire) were using similar decoration, which they combined with a style of design derived from Cubism.

From Vienna, Poiret went on to Budapest and then to Moscow, where a Russian draughtsman, Romain de Tirtoff, sketched the fashions which the couturier showed. A few years later, Erté, as this young man called himself, would be one of the brilliant artists from whom Poiret commissioned designs.

'In Berlin', Poiret wrote, 'I spent whole days visiting modern interiors, built and arranged with such a wealth of new ideas that I had seen nothing like them at home . . . . I dreamed of creating in France a movement of ideas that would be capable of propagating a new mode in decoration and furnishing.' On his return to Paris, Poiret established the Atelier Martine, where he installed about a dozen young girls and encouraged them to make sketches of plants and animals, without any adult guidance or tuition. The fresh, naive results were then converted into repeating fabric designs and printed in Normandy. Poiret used them for both dress and furnishing fabrics. Raoul Dufy also designed a number of fabrics and wallpapers for the Atelier Martine.

The Atelier Martine produced furniture, some of it designed by Pierre Fauconnet, 'an artist of indescribable charm' according to Poiret. A Martine armchair, with sides in a grid pattern, was certainly derived from the work of Hoffmann, and some of the Martine metalwork owed much to the designs of Dagobert Peche. But the overall freshness and gaiety of a Martine interior, at once naive and urbane, was a new phenomenon which was indeed 'capable of propagating a new mode in decoration and furnishing'. Two features introduced by the Atelier Martine became particularly fashionable during the 1920s. One was the bar in the private house, and the other was the sunken bathtub. The actor Sacha Guitry ordered the first bathtub, which was lined with gilt mosaic. 'Enough of privation!' he cried.

In 1913, Jacques-Emile Ruhlmann caused a sensation with the furniture which he exhibited at the Salon d'Automne. Made of exotic woods and inlaid with ivory and ebony, it had all the elegance and craftsmanship of work by the master *ébénistes* of the late eighteenth century. Yet it was unmistakably modern. Art Deco was born.

Before the outbreak of the First World War, not only had the characteristics of the Deco style been formulated, but also the social attitudes which demanded it had been moulded. The new rich, their numbers to be swelled by profits from the forthcoming Armageddon, had rebelled against the repressive morality preached by churches and promulgated by rulers. For instance, the tango: this was disliked by the Kaiser and banned in Munich; rejected by the Pope for a stately peasant dance; prohibited, along with the one-step, by the Tsar; and denounced by the clergy of Paris who called it a 'disgusting dance of low origin'. Yet everywhere in the years before the war the tango was danced nevertheless. In the four years of deadly warfare the bastions of moral authority fell. The survivors cried: 'Enough of privation!'

Left Drawing by George Barbier of Nijinsky in *Schéhérazade*, around 1910. Barbier's style clearly owes much to the graphic designs of Aubrey Beardsley.

Opposite Aubrey Beardsley's *Ex Libris*, 1897. The scandalous flavour of Beardsley's drawings reflected a feeling of revolt against Victorian prudery, and during the early decades of the twentieth century his work inspired artists everywhere who strove to liberate themselves from accepted mores and established taste.

Right Fashion-plate by Georges Lepape for Paul Poiret, 1911. Beardsley's malign wit is absent, but otherwise Lepape's style, which looks forward directly to Art Deco, was largely derived from the English artist's work of the 1890s. Beardsley's designs, reproduced in *The Studio*, were widely disseminated.

Above Willow Tea Rooms,
Glasgow, designed by
Charles Rennie Mackintosh,
1898–1904. Mackintosh, a
Scottish architect and
designer, created exteriors
and interiors which
prefigured Art Deco not only
in many of their decorative
motifs, but also in the
integrated style applied to
every detail of the building.

Above and right 78 Derngate, Northampton, transformed in 1916. Mackintosh's style became ever more geometrical and particularly Deco in feeling is the stepped fire-surround.

Above The building designed
by Joseph Maria Olbrich,
1897–8, for the Secession's
exhibitions was a clear
expression of the ideals
formulated by this group of
Viennese artists. The
building is composed of
geometrical blocks;
ornament has been stylized
and confined to small areas.

Right Page from *Ver Sacrum,*
the journal of the Vienna
Secession. The typography
and decoration are derived
from Aubrey Beardsley's
work, with which the
Viennese artists would have
been familiar through the
pages of *The Studio*.

Left and opposite Palais Stoclet, the Brussels home of the coal magnate Adolphe Stoclet, designed by Josef Hoffmann and built between 1905 and 1911. The commission included not only the design of the house and grounds, but also the interiors, including furniture, textiles and cutlery. Gustav Klimt, Koloman Moser, Carl Otto Czeschka and other members of the Wiener Werkstätte worked on the mansion, which became, in its unity of design and use of luxurious materials, the progenitor of many decorative schemes in the Deco style. Particularly characteristic of Art Deco are the floral patterns, the geometrical articulation and the integration of sculpture into the interior design.

Right Cabinet in white-painted wood, designed by Otto Prutscher, around 1910. Prutscher, together with Eduard Wimmer, introduced a more relaxed style to the geometrical designs of the Secession artists. The clean contours and the fluting on its feet and doors make this cabinet a direct precursor of much Art Deco furniture.

Left China figurine by Michael Powolny, around 1905. Powolny, who had been one of the founders of both the Secession and the Wiener Werkstätte, started the Wiener Keramik studio in 1905 with Berthold Löffler. This piece, painted black and white, reflects the graphic style of Aubrey Beardsley.

Above Table-lamp in beaten copper, designed by Josef Hoffmann, around 1905. Hoffmann's designs of this period were revolutionary in the rigorous geometry of their shapes and the total absence of ornament.

Right Elevated tray in white-painted metal designed by Josef Hoffmann in 1905.

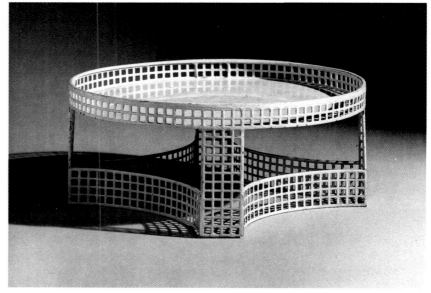

Right Woolworth Building,
New York, 1913, designed by
Cass Gilbert. Despite its
Gothic-Revival detailing, this
skyscraper, with its strong
vertical and horizontal
articulation, looks forward to
many American buildings of
the 1920s, such as the
Chicago Tribune Tower.

Left Reliance Building, Chicago, 1890–5, designed by Daniel H. Burnham and J. W. Root. The articulation of this building is a direct reflection of its metal-frame construction and the decoration simply reinforces the lines of the windows.

Above **Hanging lamp with leaded glass shade, designed by Louis Comfort Tiffany. The style of this lamp, perhaps derived from an American Indian motif, is virtually pure Deco, and yet the design was conceived as early as 1889.**

Left **Tall clock, mahogany with brass inlay, 1912, designed by George Grant Elmslie, who worked for a time in the same architect's office as Frank Lloyd Wright. The feet of this clock indicate the affinity between American designers at the turn of the century and the English Arts and Crafts movement. Otherwise, the design and finish of this piece foreshadow the Deco style.**

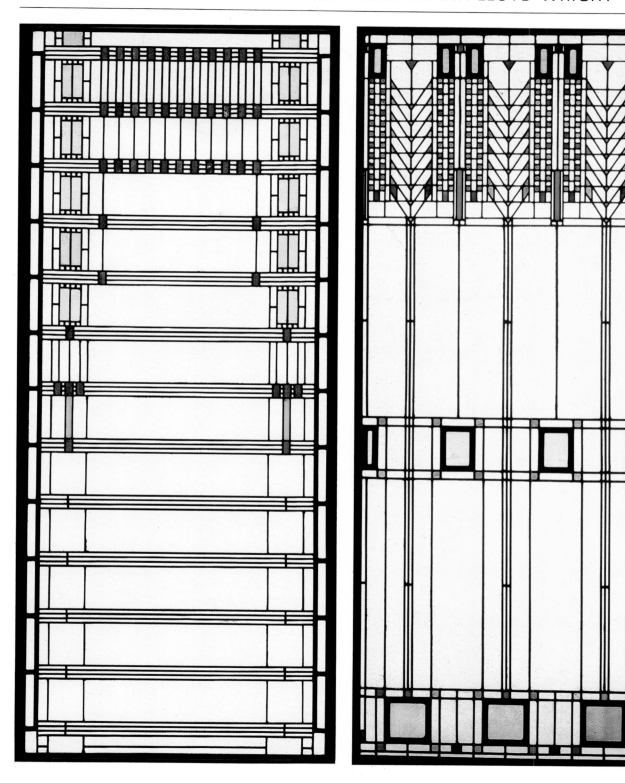

Left Leaded glass doors designed by Frank Lloyd Wright, executed by Linden Glass, for the D.D. Martin house, Buffalo, New York, around 1904. As early as the first years of the century, Wright had outgrown his schooling in the progressive ornamental style of Victorian England; this decorative design has the refined, geometrical formalism found in much later Art Deco.

Right Chair designed by
Bruno Schmitz, around 1905.
Strongly influenced earlier by
the Belgian Art Nouveau
designer Henry van de Velde,
Schmitz demonstrates here
the pervasive power of
Hermann Muthesius's call for
a neo-classical style in
German design. The elegant
simplicity was part of the
German contribution to the
Deco style.

Left Stoneware vase
designed by C. J. van der
Hoef for the Amstelhoek
pottery in Amsterdam, around
1900. The simple, restrained
ornament contrasts with the
more elaborate decoration of
Rozenburg porcelain which
was being produced in
Holland at the same time.
Van der Hoef was one of a
group of designers
associated with the architect
H. P. Berlage.

Left Interiors exhibited by the Deutscher Werkbund at the 1910 Salon d'Automne in Paris, the dining-room *(above)* by Adelbert Niemeyer and the lady's bedroom *(below)* by Karl Bertsch. What made a deep impression on French designers was the unity of conception which these rooms displayed: the notion of the 'ensemble' became an important element in the Art Deco style. The octagonal and oval shapes, and the decorative motif of clusters of flowers, also found a place in the Deco vocabulary.

In 1911, Paul Poiret introduced a range of perfumes which were sold under the brand name 'Rosine'. The packaging *(below)*, a large part of their appeal, he designed himself. The interior of the shop where the perfumes were sold *(opposite)* was furnished and decorated by the Atelier Martine, the design studio opened by Poiret in 1912. The geometrical simplicity of the furniture reflects the couturier's first-hand acquaintance with German and Austrian design.

Above Flats in Rue Franklin, Paris, designed by Auguste Perret, 1902–3. The rectangular appearance of the facade reflects the concrete construction of the building, and the flowery patterning of the maiolica tiles is an early manifestation of a favourite Deco motif.

Right A fashion-plate for the couturier Paquin, 1913, drawn by George Barbier. This is another instance of Beardsley's influence on French draughtsmen during the first quarter of the twentieth century.

Création PAQUIN

Right Costume design by Natalia Goncharova for a Russian peasant woman in *Le Coq d'Or,* a Ballets Russes production of 1914. The impact of Serge Diaghilev's Ballets Russes on Parisian artists can hardly be overestimated. The combination of bright colours, naive designs and the dancers' lascivious movements exactly caught the mood of French society, already titillated by Poiret's bold fashions.

Above: La Biche Blanche, a
drawing by Georges Lepape,
1916. A powerful influence
on Lepape and Barbier was
the decor designed for the
Ballets Russes by Bakst and
Benois, whose colourful sets
and costumes were an
inspiration to many of the Art
Deco designers.

Above Costume design by
Léon Bakst for a Chinaman in
The Sleeping Princess. Bakst
and Benois' designs for the
Ballets Russes productions
at the Châtelet Theatre in
Paris fuelled the craze for the
Orient that took hold of Paris
and made a considerable
contribution to Art Deco.

Left China box designed by Pavel Janák, 1914. Janák was a Czechoslovak architect and designer influenced by both Cubist painting and the decorative style developed by the Wiener Werkstätte.

Below Clock, 1913, designed by the Czechoslovak architect Josef Gočár for Otto Boleška, an actor with the National Theatre in Prague. Here elements of Cubism, German Expressionism and Viennese design have been blended to form a unique, coherent style which looks forward to Art Deco.

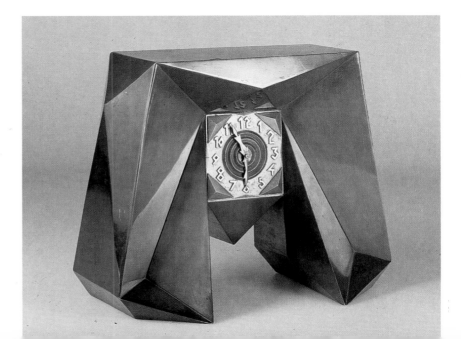

Left Corner-cupboard by Jacques-Emile Ruhlmann, 1916, in amboyna wood with ivory and ebony inlay. The furniture which Ruhlmann exhibited at the Salon d'Automne in 1913 caused a sensation. Rich materials and fine craftsmanship, as well as his stylish designs, were Ruhlmann's contribution to Art Deco.

Opposite left Cover of the catalogue for the 9th Salon de la Société des Artistes Décorateurs, 1914, by François-Louis Schmied. This drawing demonstrates the impact of German and Austrian design on French artists before the First World War: there are elements here of Deutscher Werkbund neo-classicism and Wiener Werkstätte geometrical pattern.

Opposite right Cover of the catalogue for the 10th Salon de la Société des Artistes Décorateurs, 1919, by Henri Rapin. In comparison with the illustration opposite, it can be seen how, as a result of the anti-German feeling aroused by the First World War, the decorative style has been gallicized. Rapin became one of the leading Art Deco designers, responsible for much of the decoration on Sèvres porcelain during the 1920s.

'English visitors to the Paris Exhibition might be divided into two types; one, the persons who spent a day at the Exhibition on the return journey from a Swiss holiday, and the other, the more serious people, who spent a week or more really studying the Exhibition.

'The Swiss holiday type, with their eyes thoroughly out of focus from staring at the mountains, misunderstood and disliked nearly all they saw in their rush round. The serious people, though critical and somewhat startled, were, on the whole, deeply impressed; and with good reason, for the Exposition des Arts Décoratifs was one of *the* events of modern art history.'

These words were written by George Sheringham, a British artist, shortly after the event, yet he cannot be accused of over-enthusiasm. The Exposition Internationale des Arts Décoratifs et Industriels Modernes, held in Paris during 1925, from which the Art Deco style derived its name, remains unquestionably the most important international exhibition of the applied arts in this century, and it must be ranked among the many cultural achievements that emerged on the Parisian scene during the 1920s—'les Années Folles'. In painting, Picasso, Matisse, Miró and Ernst were exhibiting in Paris some of their finest works. In literature, Proust, Cocteau, Colette, Mauriac, Gide, Eluard and Aragon all had books published in the course of the decade. Music by Ravel, Satie and Poulenc was first performed in Paris. Audiences watched the premières of Gance's *Napoléon,* Dreyer's *La Passion de Jeanne d'Arc* and Buñuel's *Le Chien Andalou*; *rayogrammes* were invented by Man Ray in 1923. Brancusi sculpted his *Leda* in 1920, André Breton published the Surrealist Manifesto in 1924—both in Paris.

Sisley Huddleston, the Paris correspondent of *The Times* during most of that fecund decade, recalled some of its characteristic talking-points: 'Cubist and other queer paintings ... typewriters ... cocaine, silk stockings ... Freudism ... unnatural vices ... aeroplanes and cocktails.' Parisian life was effervescent, bubbling with liberation and innovation. 'Paris was decked with flags for ten years after the Armistice,' wrote Maurice Sachs, 'I remember that decade like a perpetual Fourteenth of July.' There was a rugged determination to drown unhappy memories of the war years, the bereavement and the austerity. As well as cocktails, from America there came movies and jazz. Harry's Bar was opened in 1918, and every fashionable café had its pianist.

The commercial viability of modern art had been discovered by Ambrose Vollard and Daniel Kahnweiler before the war, and during the 1920s the Ecole de Paris was booming. Artists flocked to the French capital and congregated in Montparnasse. Maurice Sachs thought that the public was endeavouring to make amends for the neglect suffered by such artists as Rimbaud, Gauguin and Van Gogh. 'For fear of passing by a "genius",' he wrote, 'we will soon be so encumbered with them that one will be able to walk along with a lantern saying: "I'm looking for a man with no talent."' From this multitude of artists thronging Paris, the manufacturers and entrepreneurs of the French decorative arts could draw a limitless supply of designs. Many of those who aspired to the success of a Picasso or a Matisse could, meanwhile, make a reasonable living this way. 'If you wanted in the mid-twenties to make a living in Paris as an artist,' recalled Simon Lissim, a young Russian painter at that time, 'you had to work in all areas, and mostly in those of the Decorative Arts.' Consequently, there were close connections between the worlds of the fine and decorative arts, a situation which Paul Poiret had also helped to create by employing artists as designers. Symbolic of this proximity between different fields of artistic endeavour was the editorial 'office' of the magazine *Mobilier et Décoration,* which was run by Edmond Honoré and his wife from a table at the Café aux Deux Magots in the Boulevard Saint-Germain; there they sat each evening from five to seven-thirty discussing projected features with contributors, while at nearby tables sat André Derain and the sculptor Charles Despiau.

With a detectable note of envy, the English silversmith Henry Wilson wrote in the mid-1920s: 'Numbers of French artists have had the time of their lives, with fair pay and unending opportunity of realizing dreams, on the flat or in the round, all urged by friendly rivalry to do their best and hardest.' The artists-cum-designers did not have to restrict their activities to a single area; in fact, many of them turned their hand to a variety of applied arts. Lissim, for example, designed stage décor, porcelain, textiles, glass, window-displays, book illustrations, posters, flatware, jewellery, wallpapers, screens, playing-cards and even flags for a shipping company. Robert Bonfils was a French painter who became one of the organizers of the 1925 Exhibition; he also designed a poster for it, and the cover of the official catalogue. In addition, he designed bookbindings, textiles for the firm of Bianchini Férier and porcelain for the Sèvres factory.

This versatility among designers had one significant result: it promoted a universal style. French designers, tradesmen and critics had been shocked by the immense success which the German decorative arts had gained with the public when they had been exhibited at the Salon d'Automne in 1910. It had been recognized that a crucial factor had been the total effect induced by a stylistic cohesion, encompassing everything from curtains to carpets, from furniture to metalwork. *'Ensemble'* and *'ensemblier'* had quickly become catchwords in the literature of the French decorative arts. The officials in the Ministère des Beaux-Arts noted the co-ordinating role that had been played by Hermann Muthesius in the development of German design, and as soon as the war was over they set out to promote a unified style for the decorative arts in France. Louis Süe, a painter and architect who had begun his career as *ensemblier* in 1911, was commissioned to design the Cénotaphe de l'Etoile with the painter André Mare. Edgar Brandt, a metalworker who would become one of the luminaries of the 1925 Exhibition, made a war memorial at Douaumont.

If a single style was going to be adopted in France during the post-war years, everyone must have known its likely characteristics. As a

Cover by Robert Bonfils of the official catalogue of the Paris Exhibition, 1925. The leaping deer, the running, lightly-clad female figure and the basket of flowers are quintessential Deco. Bonfils was a member of the Exhibition organizing committee.

reminder, the Salon d'Automne of 1919 featured an interior by Poiret's Atelier Martine, the walls decorated in orange, gold and black, and the furniture fitted with silk tassels for handles. The same year, George Barbier, also from the Poiret stable, was commissioned by Cartier to design a collection of jewellery. Jacques-Emile Ruhlmann, whose furniture had first been acclaimed in 1913, set up a company, Ruhlmann et Laurent, in 1919 at 27 Rue de Lisbonne; and that year, too, Louis Süe and André Mare founded the Compagnie des Arts Français, whose object was to create decorative ensembles complete with mural paintings and sculpture.

In 1921 Süe et Mare published a book, *L'Architectures,* and the new style in the decorative arts was further promoted by a series of monographs on contemporary French designers issued by the Ministère des Beaux-Arts. The government also supported the movement by granting large subsidies to state-owned factories like Sèvres and Gobelins, and in 1924 the Union Centrale des Arts Décoratifs (a government body) held an exhibition with the theme of a lady's boudoir, where designers had to create an ensemble of harmonizing furniture, hangings, carpets, light-fittings and objets d'art. It was a dress rehearsal for the 1925 Exhibition.

The year 1925 was not particularly beneficent to France. The Syrians revolted against French rule and Riff tribesmen invaded French Morocco. At home, the value of the franc was plummeting while taxation soared. Paris, however, put on a brave face for the visitors to the Exhibition. Both the Ballets Russes and the Ballets Suédois had seasons at Paris theatres that year, and Josephine Baker's Revue Nègre was all the rage. The galleries mounted exhibitions of their artists' work hoping to attract the tourists and, of course, the hotels, cafés and restaurants were crammed.

An international exhibition of decorative art had been mooted before the war, but the proposal had been repeatedly shelved, at first because of the lead which the Germans had assumed in 1910, and then because of the hostilities. By 1925, the French had occupied the Ruhr, Germany's industrial heartland, for two years, and feelings against 'les sales Boches' still ran high: a ban on Wagner's work at the Paris Opéra had only recently been lifted, and in September *L'Illustration* ran an article pointing out the threat of Germany's numerical superiority and her resurgent industries. Germany was not invited to take part in the 1925 Exhibition. The government of the USA declined an invitation to participate in the Exhibition, ostensibly on the grounds of hard-headed economics. Asia was only represented by China and Japan, Africa only by French possessions. For some reason, Norway did not take part.

The site of the Exhibition was in the centre of Paris. It embraced the Grand Palais, the Cours La Reine, the Pont Alexandre III and, on the left bank of the Seine, the Esplanade des Invalides. Most of the pavilions were constructed in plaster on wooden frames, a good surface for mural painting and low-relief sculpture. No trees were cut down, and each of the larger pavilions was surrounded by its own garden. Water from the Seine supplied several fountains, many of them illuminated at night, when the scene was also enlivened by brightly lit restaurants and night-clubs temporarily situated on barges in the river; 'Citroën' was spelt out in coloured lights on the Eiffel Tower. Paul Poiret chose to exhibit in three *péniches* (barges) which he named *Amours, Délices* and *Orgues*. Decorated by the Atelier Martine, they featured mural decorations printed on linen from designs by Raoul Dufy manufactured by Bianchini Férier.

Three names constantly recur in the pages of the Exhibition's official catalogue: Brandt, Lalique, Ruhlmann. Edgar Brandt established his metal-workshops at Vierzon in 1919, and he collaborated with the architect Louis Favier, who provided him with most of his designs. Brandt was a superb technician, knowing how to use various thicknesses of iron to produce different nuances of colour, and using the recently developed technique of autogenous welding so that he could combine iron elements with copper, bronze and other alloys in his compositions; he also equipped his workshops with power-hammers, which had just been invented. Several pavilions at the Exhibition included decorative panels, gates or screens in iron manufactured by him and he had his own stand on the Esplanade des Invalides. But his masterpiece in 1925 was probably the Porte d'Honneur, the main entrance to the Exhibition by the Grand Palais.

René Lalique was also a fine technician. He had concentrated on the production of glass since 1914, when he opened a workshop at Combs-la-Ville; after the war he set up a factory in Alsace. He developed his own, very sophisticated techniques of moulding, colouring, acid-etching and sand-blasting glass, as well as being responsible for most of the designs. The Pavillon Lalique was decorated with bas-reliefs in glass and inside there was a display of his work, ranging from drinking-glasses and scent-bottles produced in series to *pièces uniques*. Sculpted glass panels by Lalique were incorporated in the Porte d'Honneur, and there was a fountain, in the form of a glass obelisk which was illuminated at night, on the Esplanade des Invalides. For the Sèvres pavilion, Lalique created a dining-room with a coffered ceiling in glass, and on the Parfumerie Française stand in the Grand Palais there was a glass sculpture by Lalique in the form of a fountain.

For many, the furniture of Jacques-Emile Ruhlmann is the epitome of Art Deco. The large flat surfaces, exquisitely veneered in exotic woods and inlaid with mother-of-pearl, ivory and ebony, the well-proportioned masses, the elegant contours, all justify the praises that have been lavished upon his work. At the 1925 Exhibition Ruhlmann displayed his wares in his own pavilion, called L'Hôtel d'un Collectionneur, which was modelled on the house he had commissioned for himself from the architect Pierre Patout. Here he surrounded magnificent examples of his furniture with objets d'art from the studios of others. There was sculpture by Bourdelle, Despiau and Joseph Bernard, murals by Jean Dupas, iron gates by Brandt, pottery by Lenoble and Decœur, *pâte de verre* by Décorchemont, silver by

Puiforcat, marquetry by Rapin, a carved ivory vase by Mme O'Kin and lacquer work by Dunand and Legrain. He also exhibited a bookcase in metal made by Raymond Subes, a metalworker second only to Brandt. Ruhlmann, like Brandt, took advantage of recent technical developments; he exploited the qualities of the newly introduced plywood which, because it did not warp, allowed him to design his furniture with large, flat, veneered surfaces.

L'Ambassade Française was erected on the Esplanade des Invalides, and, as its name implies, it was sponsored by the state. The Ministère des Beaux-Arts made a generous grant to the Societé des Artistes Décorateurs to furnish and decorate the rooms of an imaginary ambassador's residence. The list of artists involved reads like a roll of honour of French Art Deco. The entrance-hall was designed by Robert Mallet-Stevens, the smoking-room and the gymnasium by Francis Jourdain. One critic referred to this smoking-room as 'a magnificently barbaric harmony of colour'. On the floor there was an orange rug; furniture was covered in black lacquer by Jean Dunand, and the ceiling was laid in silver leaf with accents of red lacquer. A white ceramic figure of Jean Borlin, the leading dancer with the Ballets Suédois, modelled by Jan and Joël Martel, stood on a cupboard, and there was a screen lacquered by Dunand after a design by Lambert-Rucki.

In the dining-room of L'Ambassade there was a china service, decorated with a design by Henri Rapin, surrounding a silver centrepiece by Jean Puiforcat. Chairs by Jules Leleu graced the music-room and the salon. In the latter room, there were silk wall-hangings designed by Edouard Bénédictus, with motifs of fountains and flowers, manufactured by Bianchini Férier. Léon Jallot and his son Maurice provided the furniture for a reception room and the ambassador's bedroom. A *bureau-bibliothèque* featured the more restrained forms of Pierre Chareau's furniture, including a large pedestal writing-table veneered with rosewood; this stood on a circular carpet designed by Jean Lurçat. In the *chambre de madame* there was the curvaceous furniture, covered with shagreen and inlaid with ivory, created by André Groult; on a chest of drawers was placed a sculpture by Roger de la Fresnaye, and on the wall an oval portrait by Marie Laurençin.

An antechamber in L'Ambassade Française was furnished and decorated by Paul Follot with the collaboration of the studio Pomone, of which he was the director. Four of the principal department stores in Paris had opened decorating studios: Au Printemps had led the way with its Atelier Primavera which was directed by Mme Chauché-Guilleré. The Galeries Lafayette had started La Maîtrise in 1921 under the direction of Maurice Dufrène. Bon Marché had followed two years later with Pomone, and the last was Studium-Louvre whose designers included Djo Bourgeois and Etienne Kohlmann. These four studios, offering their customers everything to decorate their homes in the fashionable Art Deco style—from complete suites of furniture to dinner-plates and cushion-covers—propagated the concept of the ensemble. A patron of Ruhlmann or Dunand had to be very, very rich, but to have one of the department stores provide the décor it was only necessary to be well off.

In two respects, the decorating studios realized the concepts of Hermann Muthesius from the first decade of the twentieth century, which had accounted for the success of the German exhibits at the Salon d'Automne in 1910. First, the designers in each studio would work on all sorts of items. For instance, Maurice Dufrène designed carpets and textiles, as well as furniture, for La Maîtrise, and Claude Lévy, who worked for Primavera, designed both pottery and textiles. The decoration of a room was consequently harmonious and objects placed there would blend agreeably. Second, Muthesius's enthusiasm for co-operation between art and industry would have been gratified by the relationships between the studio designers and the manufacturing firms. Claude Lévy's designs for pottery were executed by the Longwy factory, and the firm of Lorthiois-Leurent et Cie wove the textiles designed by Paul Follot for Pomone.

The Compagnie des Arts Français, set up by Louis Süe and André Mare in 1919, was extensively represented at the 1925 Exhibition. The style of their work was distinctly Art Deco, though they eschewed the revolutionary or the modish. Their object was to create ensembles which were 'serious, logical, hospitable', and they found inspiration in traditional French styles. Appropriately, they were commissioned to design the Salle des Fêtes in the Grand Palais, the acme of architectural historicism.

Süe et Mare also designed and decorated the Museum of Contemporary Art at the Exhibition. In the form of a classical rotunda, the Museum was a showcase for the products of the Compagnie des Arts Français. For instance, one of the members, Roger de la Fresnaye, exhibited a ceramic figure of Eve, glazed white on a black wooden plinth. Another, the painter Luc-Albert Moreau, was represented by a portrait in oils of Grock the clown. There were several examples of furniture by Süe et Mare, made of fine woods and often embellished with marble, gilding and bronze mounts. The painter and illustrator André Marty, who belonged to the Compagnie des Arts Français, showed some screens covered in printed fabrics; these were in the Pavillon Fontaine, which was also arranged by Süe et Mare. One of the screens, entitled *Plein Air*, composed and coloured in an eighteenth-century manner, depicted a very contemporary picnic, with the ladies fashionably tubular, a man in shirt-sleeves with the current gleaming hairstyle, an automobile, a yacht, a motor-boat and the ubiquitous greyhound (or is it a borzoi?). The screen is the quintessence of the twenties image.

Three important French firms with long traditions of quality and style exhibited in 1925. The goldsmiths and silversmiths Christofle, founded in the 1820s, who showed tableware in hammered silver, had commissioned designs from Paul Follot, Süe et Mare and the Danish designer Christian Fjerdingstad. The Baccarat glassworks, founded in 1765, shared a pavilion with Christofle. Their exhibits also revealed efforts to meet contemporary stylistic demands, particularly the chandelier in the form of a fountain, a recurring Deco motif. The third French company with a long-established reputation was Sèvres. In their own faience-clad pavilion, they showed a wide variety of porcelain and stoneware. Henri Rapin designed furniture inlaid with Sèvres tiles and an illuminated bronze and porcelain fountain for the Salon des Lumières, one of the rooms in the pavilion. Porcelain models of animals, sculpted by Gaston Le Bourgeois, were to be found in the pavilion's garden.

In the Pavillon Limoges the porcelain manufacturers of that city showed their products. Predominant was the stand of the Haviland firm, which exhibited tableware decorated with designs by Suzanne Lalique, the glassmaker's daughter, and Jean Dufy, the painter's brother. Elsewhere, the Daum glass factory showed work in an up-to-date style, including coloured glass shades on metal lampstands made by Edgar Brandt.

At the other end of the scale from the large manufacturers were the individual artist-craftsmen. Some of them showed their work on the stand of Georges Rouard, at whose gallery in the Avenue de l'Opéra they regularly exhibited. Here was glass made by André Thuret and Henri Navarre at their workshops in Bagneux, near Fontainebleau, enamelled glass by Marcel Goupy, *pâte de verre* by Francois-Emile Décorchemont who was to marry Rouard's daughter two years later, and studio pottery by Emile Decœur and Emile Lenoble. Jean Puiforcat had his own stand where he showed his silver, designed in geometrical shapes and often embellished with handles in rosewood or lapis lazuli.

A richness of materials, a range of shapes and a vocabulary of decorative motifs characterized the French exhibits in 1925. Furniture was often lacquered, covered in shagreen or veneered with exotic woods such as macassar and amboyna; inlays included ivory, ebony and mother-of-pearl. Glass was embellished with metal-foil inserts or bubbles; sometimes it was tinted or opalescent, sometimes enamelled in bright colours. Much of the pottery was covered with a crackled white glaze, giving clarity and sparkle to the coloured decoration which was applied over it. Clarity was also a characteristic of the shapes seen at the 1925 Exhibition. Three-dimensional objects were treated as an assembly of planes. The octagon and the oval were favourite motifs, as well as lissom figures, and blossoms and fruits were packed densely into bands of ornament or geometric shapes. Similarly, sunbursts and fountains were formalized, whether in wrought iron or on textiles.

Deer were another favoured motif. One leapt across Robert Bonfils's cover of the official catalogue; another plunged through the woods on a vase from La Maîtrise. A herd of them circles a Pomone coffee-service, and Paul Follot designed a hand-printed linen called 'Les Biches' where they sit in groups among leaves and cacti. Like greyhounds, they were highly esteemed fauna during the twenties.

To a great extent, Art Deco owes its svelte, elegant image to the Paris couturiers. Unlike the English Arts and Crafts movement whose founding fathers were moralizing socialists, the Wiener Werkstätte which was led by theorizing architects, or the Deutscher Werkbund whose instigation came from government and industrial circles, French Art Deco was spawned by the luminaries of the world of fashion. At about the same time as one leading couturier, Paul Poiret, was launching the Atelier Martine and supervising the style of its every production, another, Jacques Doucet, began patronizing designers such as Paul Iribe, Eileen Gray and Pierre Legrain who created for him one of the earliest Art Deco environments. After the First World War, Jeanne Lanvin, who had progressed from designing children's clothes to being recognized as one of the leaders of *haute couture*, opened Lanvin Décoration, an interior decorating business for which she herself provided many of the designs. For her own apartments in Rue Barbet de Jouy she commissioned designs from Armand-Albert Rateau, whose bronze furniture in the form of birds and animals is unique among Art Deco creations. She entrusted Rateau with the direction of Lanvin Décoration which, between 1920 and 1925, designed and executed the interior of the Théâtre Daunou; Jean Dunand and the sculptor Paul Plumet worked on the project.

Underlying the important part that the couturier played in the formation of a decorative style were the growing affluence and independence of European and American women during the first quarter of this century. Apart from the increasing ideological pressure for the emancipation of women, the First World War provided them with the opportunity to shoulder responsibilities traditionally under-taken by the men who were away fighting, many of them never to return. French designers and decorators were quick to respond to the new importance that women had assumed, and they directed their work at them. Besides the obvious stylistic difference, what separates the 1925 Paris Exhibition from those of 1900 or 1889 is the attention which was paid to feminine taste, virtually for the first time. In the Pavillon d'Elégance were displayed gowns, coats, hats, shoes and underwear from such houses as Jenny, Paquin, Lanvin, Worth, Callot Sœurs, Vionnet and Patou. The pavilion was decorated by Jeanne Lanvin. There were lacquered screens by Jean Dunand and the furniture was by Armand-Albert Rateau. Particularly successful were the stylized figures on which the garments were displayed; modelled by Vigneau-Siégal, they were painted gold, silver, olive-green or black.

As well as *haute couture*, displays of jewellery and scent at the 1925 Exhibition were aimed specifically at women. Boucheron and Cartier vied with each other in ornamenting the ladies of the *nouveaux riches*, who were unable to bedeck themselves with family heirlooms. All the leading *ensembliers* exhibited at least one *chambre de femme;* as has been mentioned above, they had worked on the theme of a lady's boudoir for an exhibition organized the previous year by the Union Centrale des Arts Décoratifs. The dressing-table in its modern form, not just a mirror fitted on top of a table or chest of drawers, was an Art Deco creation, and at the 1925 Exhibition there were several examples with long, oval mirrors and drawers specially designed for jewellery, cosmetics and hair-styling equipment. Under feminine influence, the bathroom and kitchen became an integral part of the home's decorative scheme during the 1920s. Improvements in plumbing, central heating and domestic appliances enabled women to spend an extended proportion of their time in these two rooms, and they wanted them furnished, decorated and equipped to their taste. The full extent of the Art Deco designer's concern for the needs of the modern independent woman is revealed in drawings by Ernst Deutsch for ladies' car repair tools—screwdrivers and spanners with delicate pink handles, an oil-can with a pink tasselled atomizer like a scent-spray.

Other nations' displays at the 1925 Exhibition generally lacked the femininity of the French, but there were many signs that Art Deco had become an international style. In the Austrian pavilion, the Wiener Werkstätte, which had contributed so much to the evolution of the style, showed that none of its flair or elegance had been lost. The severe geometry of its earlier designs had given way to a more graceful decorative expression, and floral and figurative motifs adorned much of the work. Significantly, many of the younger Werkstätte designers were women, and there was a distinctly feminine touch to the pottery of Susie Singer and Vally Wieselthier, the enamels of Maria Likarz and the textiles of Olga Likarz. However, the glass from Czechoslovakia, now a republic and quite independent of Austria, reflected the Cubist manner of pre-war Prague.

From Belgium, where the Palais Stoclet was situated, came an exhibit that was the ultimate in ensembles. It was a dining-room created by Philippe Wolfers who, like Lalique, had made his name as an Art Nouveau jeweller. Wolfers chose a ten-sided polygon as his module, and the motif was repeated everywhere—as a pattern in the parquet floor, in the shape of the carpet, the table, the china and the cutlery. The drinking-glasses, manufactured by the firm of Val Saint-Lambert, were ten-sided at their rims; there was a ten-sided jardinière of silver and ivory. Both the concept and the design can be classified as Art Deco, but it is difficult to believe that the total effect did not make the French *ensembliers* shudder. Also from Belgium, Boch Frères' 'Keramis' pottery, covered in a white crackled glaze and decorated with highly stylized animals or flowers, was certainly Art Deco; most of it, however, was designed by a Frenchman, Charles Catteau.

The exhibits of the more recently established firms showing at Paris in 1925 tended to be in the Art Deco style. For instance, the art-pottery of Carter Stabler & Adams, founded in England in 1921, was decorated with hand-painted designs of stylized floral motifs—and sometimes deer—very much in the Deco idiom, particularly the work of Truda Adams. The Orrefors glassworks, in Sweden, had only started producing artistic wares in 1918, when it had been taken over by Johan Ekman. He commissioned two artists, Simon Gate and Edward Hald, to design the shapes and decoration of Orrefors glass and much of their work—the elongated figures, the stylized billowing clouds, for example—is Art Deco in feeling. The craft-workshops of Lenci, founded in 1919 by Helenschen König-Scavini, produced work in a variety of media which was exhibited in the Italian pavilion, and which is characterized by an authentic Art Deco mixture of naivety and sophistication. Another Italian enterprise, Richard-Ginori of Doccia, although founded in the eighteenth century and so hardly to be described as recent, employed a young designer Gio Ponti, who was to develop a blend of Art Deco and the Fascist style prevailing in Italy at the time.

Many of the goods displayed at the 1925 Exhibition tended to be in styles relevant to the nation that produced them, and consequently more or less remote from Art Deco. For example, several of the British exhibits were in the Arts and Crafts idiom, and most of the countries recently created by the Treaty of Versailles in 1919, such as Poland and Yugoslavia, showed work in nationalistic styles; the former appeared dowdy, the latter provincial, in comparison with the smart urbanity of French Art Deco.

The 1925 Exhibition of Decorative Art in Paris showed that Art Deco had become an established international style. The seeds of virtually every movement in the applied arts of the twentieth century since 1925 were sown that year on the banks of the Seine. There were some dissenters: Louis Aragon, the Surrealist, was disgusted by what he saw, regarding it as the triumph of rationalization. He demanded that the whole Exhibition should be blown up with dynamite, a quantity of which should be reserved to destroy the statue of Auguste Comte, the founder of Positivism, in the Place de la Sorbonne. Paul Poiret, too, was upset by the Exhibition; for him, it was 'a great disappointment'. Few of his old customers visited his *péniches* on the Seine, and in 1930 he wrote: 'I was mistaken to count on a *de luxe* clientele, for they flee from popular pleasures.' That was another significance of the 1925 Exhibition. It not only unveiled a cosmopolitan style, it made Art Deco popular taste, regardless of social status.

Ladies' tool-kit, a design sketch by Ernst Deutsch, around 1930. This drawing highlights two important aspects of Art Deco: first, it shows how designers seized the opportunities created by a variety of new technological inventions; second, it underlines the significance of the modern woman, liberated and fashion-conscious.

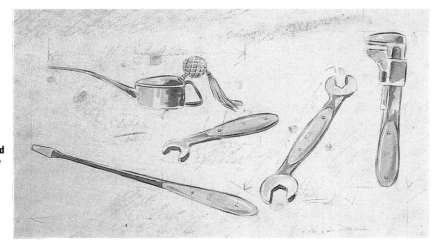

Above Porte d'Honneur, one of the main entrances to the Paris Exhibition of 1925, with ironwork by Edgar Brandt. Behind it, on the left, is the Grand Palais.

Left General view of the Paris Exhibition on the *rive droite*, with the Grand Palais in the centre. The historicism of the Grand Palais' architecture contrasts with the plainer modernity of the Exhibition pavilions.

Above: L'Europe, an illustration by George Barbier, 1920. Art Deco became the prevailing style of decorative art almost immediately after the First World War. Here, on the threshold of the decade, Barbier captures the spirit of fashionable Paris during the twenties. The *décolleté* gowns, the bobbed hair and the elegant gestures are hallmarks of new social attitudes. And, although the setting is eighteenth-century in style, the turquoise and orange colours are typical of Art Deco.

Below: The Three Graces by George Barbier, around 1920. Here Barbier shows the influence of Paul Poiret on the Art Deco style. The raised hemline and the turban adorned with feathers were both created by Poiret.

Right Bookbinding by Robert Bonfils, around 1925. Trained as a painter as well as a decorative artist, he was much in demand during the twenties. His work was to be found in no fewer than nine different classes at the 1925 Exhibition. In addition to bookbindings, posters and other graphic art, his designs were used on textiles and porcelain.

Above Illustration of a study by Pierre Chareau from Léon Moussinac's *Intérieurs*, 1924. Moussinac and others produced albums of designs for interior decoration during the twenties in the same way that Poiret had published albums illustrating his collections of *haute couture* some dozen years earlier.

Left Illustration of a studio in Paris by Süe et Mare from Léon Moussinac's *Intérieurs*, 1924. In 1919 Louis Süe and André Mare founded the Compagnie des Arts Français, a group of painters and sculptors who provided designs for room-ensembles.

Left Illustration of a bedroom by Eric Bagge from Léon Moussinac's *Intérieurs*, 1924. Bagge was noted for his textile designs, as well as providing drawings for many pieces of jewellery made in Georges Fouquet's workshops.

Right Poster for *Revue Nègre,* around 1926, designed by Paul Colin. The twenties vogue for Negro culture extended from tribal masks to jazz and Josephine Baker.

Right Paul Poiret and Josephine Baker photographed *chez* Poiret on 25 November 1925. There is a touch of irony in this zany double portrait. While Josephine Baker was the new goddess of Parisian society, Poiret, who had done so much to shape the twenties, was beginning to see his fortunes fade. By the end of the decade, he would be a pauper.

Left Backdrop to Diaghilev's *Le Train Bleu,* designed by Pablo Picasso, 1924. The masters of the Ecole de Paris — Picasso, Matisse, van Dongen, Foujita — created an atmosphere in which the decorative arts flourished. Elements of their various styles are often found in Art Deco designers' work.

Right Pont Alexandre III over the Seine, photographed during the 1925 Paris Exhibition. The bridge, which connected the two parts of the Exhibition site, was temporarily converted into a row of boutiques where a number of smaller firms and individual artist-craftsmen displayed their wares. The Oriental inspiration of the architecture and the decorations in low relief are typical of the style prevalent at the Exhibition.

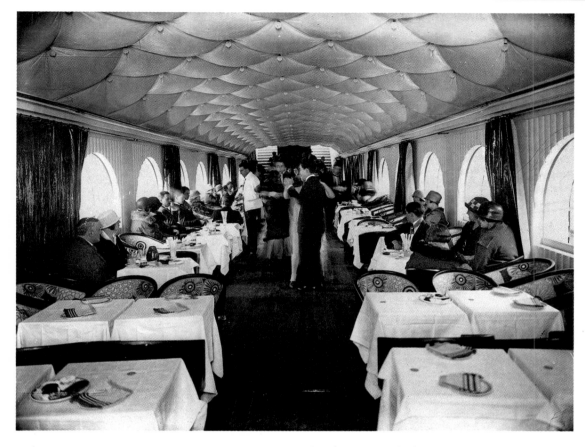

Left Dancing aboard the *péniche* (barge) *'Orgues'*, one of the three which Paul Poiret moored on the Seine during the 1925 Paris Exhibition. Poiret was disappointed with the Exhibition; few of his high-spending clients turned up and his extravagant display hastened his financial ruin.

Right The salon on the *péniche 'Amours'*. The furniture and fabrics are by the Atelier Martine, but the geometrical style of the tables and chairs, derived from Wiener Werkstätte designs of more than twenty years earlier, must have appeared rather old-fashioned by 1925.

Right: 'Les Algues' (Algae), a silvered wrought-iron standing lamp by Edgar Brandt, around 1925. Brandt, a metalworker, exploited new techniques and technology to obtain original effects of colour and depth in his ironwork. His association with Daum, the firm of glass-makers which supplied the shades for Brandt's lampstands, was highly successful; here, the watery effect in the shade complements the marine vegetation which decorates the stand.

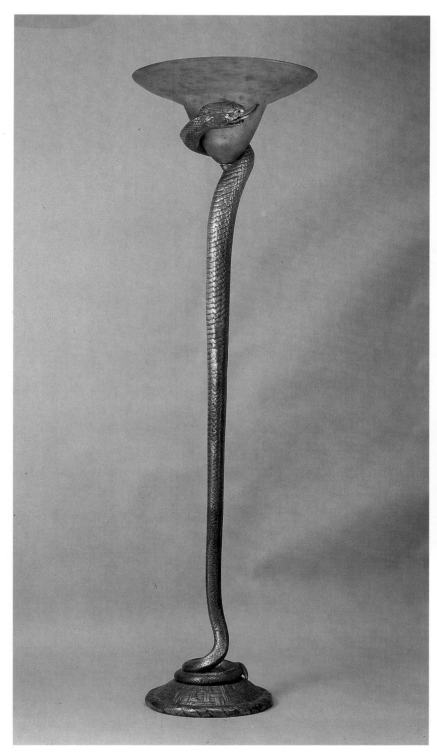

Above Chandelier in wrought iron by Edgar Brandt, with Daum shades, around 1925. Brandt was first and foremost a craftsman; most of his pieces were designed by the architect Louis Favier.

Left Standing lamp in wrought iron by Edgar Brandt, with a Daum shade, around 1925. This piece demonstrates Brandt's amazing range of patination; here the iron has been given an almost shiny finish to give the appearance of a serpent.

Above, left and right Bronze vessels by Edgar Brandt, around 1925. The designs used by Brandt developed from a style incorporating naturalistic animals to a more formal, geometrical language. The spiral became one of the most frequent motifs in his work.

Right Umbrella-stand by Edgar Brandt, around 1925.

Left Firescreen in iron and bronze by Edgar Brandt, around 1925. The technique of autogenous welding was exploited by Brandt to combine iron with other metals in a single piece.

Right Dining-room in the Sèvres pavilion at the Paris Exhibition 1925. Designed by the architect Marc Ducluzeau, this room was decorated by René Lalique. The coffered ceiling and the low-relief panels were glass; the table was laid with drinking glasses and candelabra; above the table hung a glass lamp, and below it the floor was laid with glass tiles – all manufactured by Lalique. The furniture was made by Bernel.

Left The Lalique pavilion at the Paris Exhibition, 1925. The glass fountain in the foreground was illuminated at night.

Above Vase in coloured glass by René Lalique. Acclaimed for his Art Nouveau jewellery at the turn of the century, Lalique started making glass before the First World War. During the twenties, his Art Deco style flourished; at the Paris Exhibition of 1925 he exhibited in his own large pavilion on the Cours La Reine.

Below Vase in cloudy glass by René Lalique. A wide range of techniques was exploited at Lalique's factory in Alsace. Sometimes his style is not so rigorously Deco; here the female form is treated more in the manner of Renoir.

Above Glass scent-bottle *L'Oiseau de Feu (The Firebird)* by René Lalique. As its name implies, this design was inspired by the Ballets Russes presentation of Stravinsky's ballet.

Above Desk in macassar wood and gilt-bronze by Jacques-Emile Ruhlmann, around 1926. The furniture of Ruhlmann was original in its simplicity and elegance, the workmanship was exquisite and the materials were luxurious.

Left Tea-service in silver and ivory by Jean Puiforcat, around 1930. The silversmith Puiforcat shared with Ruhlmann a delight in clean contours and rich materials. At the Paris Exhibition of 1925, some of Puiforcat's silver was displayed in Ruhlmann's Hôtel d'un Collectionneur. Both artists aspired to create functional objects that were also collectors' pieces.

Above Hôtel d'un Collectionneur which housed Jacques-Emile Ruhlmann's display at the Paris Exhibition of 1925. The Hôtel was designed by Pierre Patout and was modelled on the private house which the same architect had designed for Ruhlmann. Among the artists whose work was represented here were Bourdelle, Despiau, Bernard, Jourdain, Rapin, Puiforcat, Decœur, Lenoble, Brandt, Décorchemont and Legrain.

Right Chiffonier in macassar wood by Jacques-Emile Ruhlmann, around 1925. Although the design of this cupboard is very close to the one illustrated opposite, each example of Ruhlmann's furniture was given different decorative details, making it an individual piece.

Right Dining-room of L'Ambassade Française designed by Henri Rapin. The Ministère des Beaux-Arts made a substantial grant to the Société des Artistes Décorateurs to design and decorate an ambassadorial residence on the Esplanade des Invalides at the 1925 Paris Exhibition. Each room was assigned to one of the leading French *ensembliers*. Rapin's contribution was this dining-room, and he was also responsible for the decoration of the Sèvres dinner-service on the table. The silver centrepiece and cutlery were designed by Jean Puiforcat.

Left Smoking-room of L'Ambassade Française designed by Francis Jourdain. The black lacquer furniture was the work of Jean Dunand, who also executed the red lacquer screen designed by Lambert-Rucki.

Below: Bureau-bibliothèque of L'Ambassade Française designed by Pierre Chareau. The furniture, too, was designed by Chareau, and the circular rug by the painter Jean Lurçat.

Above Dining-room at the 1925 Paris Exhibition with furniture designed by Jules Leleu and carpets by Bruno da Silva Bruhns. Leleu ran his own furniture workshops and had a stand on the Esplanade des Invalides at the 1925 Exhibition. The rugs and carpets by da Silva Bruhns often incorporated the Greek key-pattern, although later they became more modernistic.

Left **Cupboard in burr walnut and ivory by Jules Leleu, around 1924.**

Right **Sofa by Pierre Chareau, covered with tapestry by Jean Lurçat, round 1926. Chareau's furniture designs often incorporated a subtle play of curves against straight lines.**

Left Chairs in beech and rosewood in the style of Paul Follot, around 1923. The products of the department stores' decorating studios were not as *de luxe* as the work of the top designers and craftsmen such as Ruhlmann or Dunand. But the moderately well-off could afford furniture and accessories from Pomone, La Maîtrise, Primavera and Studium-Louvre.

Below Sideboard, around 1925, designed by Maurice Dufrène who directed La Maîtrise, the decorating studio opened in 1921 by Galeries Lafayette. Dufrène had started his career as an Art Nouveau designer, but soon after 1900 he reacted against the style and was among the artists who created Art Deco. In his designs there is usually a strong feeling of traditional French elegance.

Opposite Study designed by Paul Follot, 1924. Follot was in charge of Pomone, the decorating studio opened in 1923 by the department store Bon Marché. The leading Parisian stores opened such studios to cater for a growing clientele who not only wanted furniture and decoration in the new style, but also demanded a consistency in the design of each room.

Above Salon suite in giltwood and tapestry by Süe et Mare, exhibited at the 1925 Paris Exhibition. Through their firm, the aptly named Compagnie des Arts Français, Süe et Mare aspired to create objects in the French manner. Most of their work echoes the Empire style of the early nineteenth century, but, as in these pieces of furniture, the historical ornament is paraphrased in a contemporary vernacular. The tapestry design was by Charles Dufresne.

Right Cupboard by Süe et
Mare, around 1925. The
carved tassels and *bombé*
legs are typical of the
style developed by Süe et
Mare.

Opposite Screen painted by
André Marty, exhibited by
Süe et Mare in the Pavillon
Fontaine at the 1925
Exhibition. Although
reminiscent of a painting by
Watteau, the figures and
props depicted here are
emphatically of the twenties.
Marty was a painter, fashion
designer and book illustrator
who belonged to the
Compagnie des Arts
Français.

Below Clock in gilt-bronze
on an onyx plinth by Süe et
Mare, around 1925.

Above Wall fountain
decorated with a satyr's
mask in gilt-bronze, by Süe et
Mare, around 1925.

Right Perfume bottle by Baccarat, around 1928. At the 1925 Paris Exhibition, Baccarat shared a pavilion with the goldsmiths and silversmiths Christofle. They were two of the longest-established French manufacturers, but, as this bottle shows, they successfully absorbed the Art Deco style.

Opposite Glass vase by Daum, around 1930. During the twenties much of the glassware produced by the Daum workshops at Nancy was decorated with acid-etched geometrical ornament or stylized animal and floral patterns.

The National Porcelain Manufactory at Sèvres has always been subsidized by the state, and during the twenties designs were commissioned from a wide range of artists. Most of the ware was either decorated with ornament in the Art Deco style *(right)* or painted with designs in the diluted Cubism of the Ecole de Paris *(left)*.

Above Entrance to the Pavillon de Sèvres at the 1925 Paris Exhibition, designed by the architects Pierre Patout and André Ventre.

Left **Porcelain vases by
Sèvres, 1920s.**

Right Plaque in *pâte de verre* by François-Emile Décorchemont, around 1922. The *pâte de verre* (made from powdered glass crystals, in this case) produced by Décorchemont during the twenties is notable for its high-relief carving and its wide range of colours.

Left **Stoneware bottle by Henri Simmen, around 1920. The artist-potter Simmen made many pieces with covers or stoppers carved in wood or ivory by his Japanese wife, Madame O'Kin; she exhibited a carved ivory figure in Ruhlmann's Hôtel d'un Collectionneur at the 1925 Paris Exhibition.**

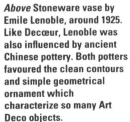

Above Stoneware vase by Emile Lenoble, around 1925. Like Decœur, Lenoble was also influenced by ancient Chinese pottery. Both potters favoured the clean contours and simple geometrical ornament which characterize so many Art Deco objects.

Above Vase in *pâte de verre* by François-Emile Décorchemont, around 1930. From 1928, Décorchemont abandoned ornament and concentrated on pure form. Lenoble, Decœur and Décorchemont all sold their wares through the gallery run by Georges Rouard, whose daughter Décorchemont married.

Left Stoneware vase by Emile Decœur, around 1925. The stoneware made by Decœur was influenced by Chinese pottery of the pre-Ming dynasties. In 1925 there was an important exhibition of ancient Chinese art in Paris.

Above and right Jewel-box and desk in rosewood and lacquered leather by Clément Mère, 1923. Trained as a painter, Mère had worked for the fashion-houses before he started making his exquisite, usually small, pieces of furniture. Here there is a distinctly Oriental feeling to both form and decoration.

Above Pair of wall-brackets by Armand-Albert Rateau, around 1925. The art of Rateau was strongly influenced by classical antiquity and the Orient. For the furniture and fittings which he made for a succession of wealthy clients, he used bronze, wood and lacquer.

Left Table-lamp in bronze and alabaster by Armand-Albert Rateau, around 1925. Animals were often incorporated in Rateau's furniture designs.

Opposite Boudoir by Armand-Albert Rateau in the apartment of the fashion designer Jeanne Lanvin, 1920—22.

Above Cigarette-cases in gold and enamel by Cartier, dating from the 1920s.

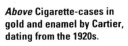

Left Pendant in jade, black onyx and diamonds by Georges Fouquet, around 1925. Oriental motifs frequently occur in Art Deco design.

Below Art Deco bangle in black onyx, diamonds and emeralds by Cartier, dating from the 1920s.

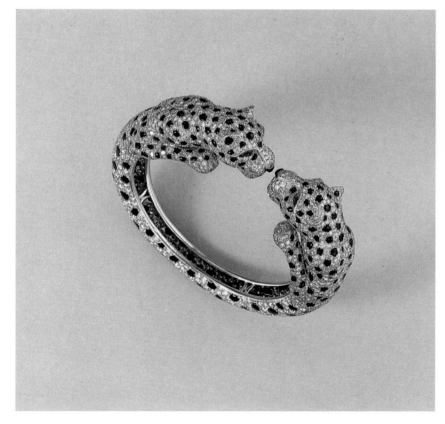

Left Czechoslovak pavilion at the 1925 Paris Exhibition, designed by the architect J. Gočár.

Left Glass bowl by Wondreje, 1925. The newly established Republic of Czechoslovakia concentrated the bulk of its display on its glass industry.

Right At the 1925 Paris Exhibition, Orrefors glass was displayed in the Swedish pavilion, designed by the architect Carl Bergsten.

Above Porcelain group, *The Triumph of Bacchus,* modelled by Giovanni Grande for Lenci, 1929. The Lenci craft-workshops in Italy, founded in 1919 by Helenschen König-Scavini, made porcelain figures which reflect the combination of naivety and sophistication which characterizes many Art Deco designs.

Above Pottery group, *The Bull,* by Harold and Phoebe Stabler for Carter Stabler Adams, 1921–4. The pottery produced by this English firm, founded in 1921, was hand-painted earthenware decorated with a variety of floral, figurative and geometrical designs in the Art Deco style.

Below Vase decorated by Susie Cooper, around 1927. The pottery decorated by Susie Cooper at this period reflects the influence of the 1925 Paris Exhibition on British artists.

Above The wares made by the Orrefors glassworks in Sweden from 1918 show an assimilation of the Art Deco style both in form and decoration. The principal artists were Edward Hald *(opposite below)* and Simon Gate *(opposite above)*.

Right Bowl designed by
Dagobert Peche. From 1903,
when the Wiener Werkstätte
was founded, Austrian
design had always been
avant-garde. This bowl of
1918 shows that Peche was
aware of the emerging Art
Deco style.

The organizers of the Paris Exhibition of 1925 stipulated that every object displayed should show 'a modern inspiration and a real originality'. In fact, the style encouraged by the Ministère des Beaux-Arts—the Art Deco of, for instance, Ruhlmann, Süe et Mare, Lalique, Brandt and the master *ensembliers*—recalled the traditional elegance of earlier French design, although it was given an up-to-date appearance and adapted to the demands of contemporary life. Above all, it was fashionable—not surprisingly, considering the influence on it of couturiers such as Poiret and Lanvin. Meanwhile, another couturier, Jacques Doucet, created through his patronage a variant of Art Deco which was derived from Cubism, African art and abstraction. The designers who worked for him were susceptible to the more doctrinaire modernism represented in Paris by the Swiss architect Le Corbusier. By the end of the 1920s, modernistic Art Deco had become the prevailing style of interior decoration, not only in France, but throughout Europe and America.

This second, modernistic strand of Art Deco was greatly influenced by the radical art movements—Futurism, De Stijl, Constructivism and the Bauhaus—that had sprung up elsewhere in Europe. In Italy, Filippo Tommaso Marinetti had drawn up the first Futurist manifesto in 1909. He was a poet who demanded that artists should cut themselves off from the past. In romantic terms he glorified the turbulence of modern life. 'We declare that the world's splendour has been enriched by a new beauty; the beauty of speed ... a roaring automobile, which seems to run like a machine-gun, is more beautiful than the *Victory of Samothrace*.' When a group of Italian painters came to apply Marinetti's principles to the visual arts, they soon found that Cubism was the most suitable language, without, however, fully comprehending either its true purpose or its achievements. But their ideas, expressed in a succession of bombastic manifestos, were much more accessible than the hermetic conundrums of Cubism.

Besides these particular references to Futurism in the work of the designers and decorators of the twenties, there are frequent allusions to the speed of modern life, one of Marinetti's favourite themes. The travel posters of Adolphe Mouron, called Cassandre, encapsulate this contemporary reverence for ever faster communications, and the same spirit, though less closely related to Futurism, infuses the car-radiator mascots made by Lalique and others.

Another major force was De Stijl, but it and Futurism had little in common. They did share a common influence, Cubism, and they both emphasized contemporaneity. Otherwise they were quite different movements, both in theory and practice, except for one further point of similarity: just as Marinetti was a forceful and much-travelled propagandist for Futurism, so the Dutch artist Theo van Doesburg proselytized for De Stijl, running an international magazine for the movement as well as visiting Berlin, Weimar and Paris to publicize its aims. De Stijl arose from discussions in neutral Holland during the First World War among some Dutch painters, including Mondrian, van Leck and van

Doesburg, and some Dutch architects, particularly J.J.P. Oud and Jan Wils, both of whom had been influenced by Frank Lloyd Wright. The Dutchmen aspired to create a style appropriate to every aspect of modern life, embracing art, architecture and the applied arts. In 1917 van Doesburg, in the first issue of the periodical *De Stijl*, claimed that such a style was 'now ripening, based on the pure equivalence of the spirit of the age and of the means of expression'.

The means of expression selected by the De Stijl artists was rigorously restricted, using only vertical and horizontal lines with the right-angle created where they cross, and, for colour, black, white and the primaries—red, yellow and blue. Of these simple elements consisted the compositions painted by Mondrian and van Doesburg during the years around the end of the First World War, and the famous red-blue chair made by Gerrit Rietveld in 1917.

Van Doesburg went to Berlin in 1920 and 1921 and Weimar in 1921, lecturing on De Stijl. At Weimar he visited the Bauhaus, Gropius's art school founded in 1919. The Bauhaus was then immersed in Expressionism and most of its work was imbued with the characteristics of peasant and primitive art. But van Doesburg began to influence both teachers and students and Marcel Breuer, a student who later became a teacher, was one of those who wholeheartedly and immediately accepted De Stijl. Chairs made by him in the early 1920s are clearly influenced by Rietveld's furniture. For a time, the editorial offices of *De Stijl* were installed at Weimar, and in 1923 a big retrospective of van Doesburg's work was held there. By that time the Dutch artist had in turn been influenced by modern ideas from Russia. Kasimir Malevich, the Russian Suprematist, had lectured at Weimar in 1922, and the following year the Hungarian Laszlo Moholy-Nagy, a Constructivist, had been appointed to the Bauhaus staff to run the *Vorkurs*, the basic introductory course for new students.

From 1923, and particularly after the school's move to Dessau in 1925 when Gropius began to develop design for industrial production, Bauhaus work took on a geometrical appearance. Furniture, metalwork, weaving and pottery were composed of circles and rectangles. From Constructivism, Moholy-Nagy brought a new attention to materials; the properties of plastic and metal particularly were investigated. Marcel Breuer developed tubular steel furniture at about the same time as Mart Stam, a young Dutch architect, was arriving at the same solution. Moholy-Nagy was equally concerned with light, and one of the most successful of the product ranges to come out of the Bauhaus were the light-fittings designed by Wilhelm Wagenfeld, Marianne Brandt and others.

Although Germany was absent from the 1925 Paris Exhibition, the Bauhaus style was becoming familiar to designers in the rest of Europe through the school's publications, which included monographs on van Doesburg and Malevich. Gropius always denied that there was such a thing as 'the Bauhaus style', but his claim seems somewhat ingenuous in the light of developments in European design during the second half of the 1920s and 1930s. There was a steady dissemination of Bauhaus ideas and personnel, particularly when the school was closed in 1933 by the Nazis.

Despite their avowed commitment to a 'modern inspiration', the commissioners of the 1925 Paris Exhibition tried, unsuccessfully, to stem this tide of modernism. Cubist art had become associated with foreigners: Picasso was Spanish, and Kahnweiler and Rosenberg, the leading dealers in Cubist paintings, were both Jews of foreign extraction. It was this chauvinism, as much as philistinism, which lay behind the order issued by the Ministère des Beaux-Arts to erect a high fence around Le Corbusier's Pavillon de l'Esprit Nouveau for the opening of the Exhibition. Similarly, a ministry official ordered the removal of decorative panels by the Cubist painters Fernand Léger and Robert Delaunay from the hall of the Ambassade Française. Nevertheless, in a boutique on the Pont Alexandre III, Robert's wife, Sonia, displayed textiles, clothes and screens which she had designed in the style of her husband's abstract paintings, which they called Simultaneism.

Theo van Doesburg actually protested to the Dutch government that nothing by De Stijl designers was included among the exhibits in the Dutch pavilion, but the arrival in Paris of De Stijl and Bauhaus ideas was clearly demonstrated by the Pavillon de l'Esprit Nouveau. Two years earlier, van Doesburg had arranged a comprehensive exhibition in Paris of De Stijl architecture in Léonce Rosenberg's Galerie de l'Effort Moderne, where Léger and Le·Corbusier regularly showed their Cubist paintings.

Modernism could be seen, too, in the Austrian pavilion where there was the *City in Space,* a suspended wooden composition designed by Friedrich Kiesler, an Austrian architect and a member of the De Stijl group. Attached to this pavilion was a conservatory of steel and glass designed by Peter Behrens, in whose office both Gropius and Le Corbusier had worked before the war. Behrens was now head of the school of architecture in Vienna, and his 1925 conservatory showed that he had kept abreast of his erstwhile assistants' ideas.

The most aggressively modern exhibit was the USSR pavilion. Painted red, with its exterior largely of glass, it was described in a British government report on the Exhibition as looking like a 'dilapidated conservatory'. It was designed by Konstantin Melnikov in the Russian Constructivist style. Within there was a workmen's club created by Alexander Rodchenko, painter, sculptor, designer and photographer, who was a follower of Vladimir Tatlin, the founding father of Russian Constructivism. Porcelain from the Leningrad factory was decorated with designs by Nicholas Suetin in the Suprematist style invented by Malevich.

Another building in the Exhibition, Robert Mallet-Stevens's Pavillon du Tourisme, showed an integration of doctrinaire modernism and the decorative Cubist style developed in Paris. The design of the pavilion itself was inspired by the Futurist architecture sketched, but never built, by Antonio Sant'Elia. In the main glass-roofed hall there was a narrow clerestory window running most of the way round, filled with stained glass in a Cubist-inspired design by Louis Barillet; on the walls were low-relief sculptures in the Cubist style by Joël and Jan Martel, twin brothers from Nantes. The furniture was designed by Francis Jourdain and Pierre Chareau.

In France the more radical form of modern design was represented during the early 1920s by the Swiss architect Le Corbusier. He expressed his ideas in two books, *Vers une architecture* (1923) and *L'Art décoratif d'aujourd'hui* (1925), and the impact they could have on a young artist has been recalled by Charlotte Perriand. She had just finished at the Ecole de l'Union Centrale des Arts Décoratifs in Paris, where she had been a pupil of Paul Follot and Maurice Dufrène. She was lent Le Corbusier's books by Jean Fouquet. 'I read them and they demolished everything,' she said later. 'Everything I had learnt and had been taught. They broke down a barrier, literally shattered it, and I was no longer enclosed.'

'Modern decorative art has no *decor*,' declared Le Corbusier. He wanted architecture, furniture and accessories, which he referred to as 'equipment', to be beautiful but unadorned. These ideas were presented in the Pavillon de l'Esprit Nouveau, which he designed himself, at the 1925 Exhibition. It was furnished with Thonet bentwood furniture and tables assembled from components made by Roneo, the office suppliers; for flower vases there were porcelain vessels used in the chemical industries. That Le Corbusier's aesthetic ideas were rooted in Cubism was shown by the presence on the walls of paintings by Picasso, Braque, Léger, Gris and Ozenfant, and by Lipchitz sculptures placed here and there. Le Corbusier pioneered tubular steel furniture in France and also introduced *casiers*, standardized cupboard units used throughout the house.

The Union des Artistes Modernes first exhibited in 1930 at the Pavillon de Marsan in Paris. Among its first members were Francis Jourdain, Robert Mallet-Stevens, Raymond Templier and Jean Fouquet. By 1930 several French designers were using metal in their furniture. Pierre Chareau, another member of the U.A.M., had designed a bedroom for Jacques Doucet and the office-library of the Ambassade Française at the 1925 Exhibition. Between 1928 and 1931 he created the Maison de Verre for Dr and Mme Jean Dalsace where tubular steel furniture was extensively deployed as well as modern light-fittings, tiled floors and movable room-dividers. Decoration was almost entirely absent.

Another seminal, modernistic interior was the 'bar sous le toit' (a play on the name of the famous Parisian night-club of the twenties, Le Bœuf sur le Toit), exhibited by Charlotte Perriand at the 1928 Salon d'Automne. On the strength of this, Le Corbusier took Charlotte Perriand into partnership, and at the following year's Salon d'Automne they exhibited a complete 'equipment of a dwelling'. The fitments and furniture were almost entirely of glass and metal; the floor was paved in heavy glass slabs and the ceiling lined in etched and cut glass. Here the simple, geometrical shapes and the unconventional materials of the modern movement in architecture and design were unashamedly displayed. During the thirties, even the masters of the Art Deco furniture *de luxe* bowed to the growing strength of modernity. Ruhlmann simplified the contours of his furniture, reduced their bulk and started using some metal and glass. Süe et Mare also pared down—and squared up—their furniture and sometimes employed modern materials such as aluminium.

Meanwhile a less polemical modernist style had started to emerge in France before the end of the First World War. At first it appeared only as decoration, and it owed much to Cubist painting. 'Cubism is a decorative art,' wrote the art dealer René Gimpel in 1930, 'though the Cubists didn't suspect this at the outset . . . . Once Cubism passes from a canvas to textiles, wallpapers or bindings, everyone understands it.' In 1917 Pierre Legrain designed some bookbindings for Jacques Doucet, in an abstract, geometrical style to blend with the couturier's collection of Cubist paintings and sculpture. Legrain's innovative use of materials, such as wood, mother-of-pearl and sharkskin, reflects collages made by Picasso and Braque a few years earlier, when they incorporated newspapers, wood and textiles in their compositions.

Doucet had sold his remarkable collection of eighteenth-century art and antiques in 1912. He moved into an apartment at 46 Avenue du Bois and proceeded to have it furnished and decorated with the best of contemporary design. At first he employed Paul Iribe, one of Poiret's protégés, who created for him an environment in a style laced with references to *ancien régime* elegance—Lalique provided a pair of glass doors, moulded in low relief with classical figures—but then, in 1914, Iribe went to the United States and Doucet entrusted the further decoration and furnishing of his apartment to Iribe's assistant, Pierre Legrain.

At about the same time, Doucet started to collect Cubist and African art and began to encourage the artist-decorators who worked for him to adopt an abstract, geometrical style. A lacquered table that he bought from Eileen Gray falls into this category; so does furniture by Paul Mergier and Jean-Charles Moreux, as well as carpets designed by Louis Marcoussis and Jean Lurçat, both painters who worked for a time in the Cubist style.

African art had inspired Picasso and was an important ingredient of Cubism. Doucet collected African masks and statues, and these in turn affected Legrain's style. He designed a stool whose form was directly borrowed from an Ashanti original, and much of his furniture has a primitive look about it. Marcel Coard, too, designed furniture for Doucet in a style inspired by African art. The austere, Cubist forms of Coard's furniture were enriched by his use of exotic materials—parchment, shagreen, lacquer, mother-of-pearl, lapis lazuli and amethyst. Gustave Miklos, a Hungarian artist who had settled in Paris in 1909 after studying at the Royal School of Decorative Art in Budapest, was a

Stoneware vase by René Buthaud, around 1930. Similar vases were exhibited by Buthaud at the 1931 Colonial Exhibition in Paris.

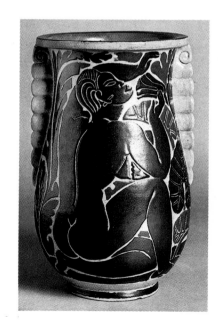

sculptor working in the Cubist style who supplied Doucet not only with sculptures but also designs for carpets and furniture. In the mid-twenties Doucet moved into a new home at Neuilly which he called the Studio, and here, in suitably contemporary surroundings, he arranged his paintings and sculptures, and—equally works of art—his carpets and furniture.

So, fostered by the patronage of Jacques Doucet and a handful of other collectors, there emerged from Cubism and African art a Deco style which was quite distinct from the flora and fauna, the stylized figures and mementos of *ancien régime* elegance characteristic of so much Art Deco. In common, the two styles had a range of bright colours—scarlet, citrus yellow, peppermint green, silver and gold, and a lot of glossy black. Some artists worked in both styles, for instance Jean Dunand whose lacquer work usually followed others' designs, and whose metal vases were decorated with formal patterns or geometrical motifs inspired by Cubism.

Several designers developed a more geometrical style as the twenties progressed; for example, Bruno da Silva Bruhns began designing rugs inspired by Berber originals in the early 1920s and by the end of the decade had started using rectangular blocks of colour and the zigzag pattern, both motifs typical of the decorative style derived from Cubism and African art. Similarly, the potter Emile Decœur stopped decorating his stoneware with stylized flowers and opted for simpler shapes with ornament restricted to a thin band of differently coloured glaze. Maurice Marinot began by decorating his glass vessels with Fauvist designs in enamels; then he began sculpting the surface of his bottles and vases with geometrical patterns. Often his work is decorated solely by manipulation of natural defects in the glass itself.

Among artists who worked almost exclusively in a geometrical style was the silversmith Jean Puiforcat, some of whose works, although functioning perfectly well as, for instance, coffee-pots or milk-jugs, appear as pieces of abstract, Cubist sculpture. French jewellery was particularly an area where arrangements of circles, semicircles, rectangles and triangles prevailed. Raymond Templier's jewellery and cigarette-cases were usually in this style, as were the designs of Gérard Sandoz. The jeweller Georges Fouquet turned to the modern style in 1922. He abandoned floral and figurative motifs, and for his abstract designs he started using different materials—onyx, coral, jade, aquamarine, amethyst and topaz. Fouquet commissioned designs from the architect Eric Bagge, the painter André Leveillé, the poster artist Adolphe Mouron (Cassandre), and the sculptor Jean Lambert-Rucki. They all worked for him in the geometrical style, sometimes, in the case of Lambert-Rucki, clearly influenced by African art. Georges Fouquet's son, Jean, often using black lacquer and translucent enamels, created jewellery of a rigid geometry; a pendant by him, made of white gold, in the form of an African mask with a line of small diamonds as the nose and two rectangles of black lacquer as the eyes, epitomizes the style. 'Pieces of jewellery', he wrote, 'must be composed of masses which are legible at a distance.'

In England, the designer's perception of a modern world gradually evolved. Vorticism was an English offshoot \of\ Futurism, and some of its adherents designed and decorated furniture and household objects for the Rebel Art Centre during the early years of the First World War. One of them, Edward McKnight Kauffer, designed posters and carpets in the Vorticist style well into the twenties, by which time Vorticist painting had perished. His wife, Marion Dorn, also designed rugs in the modernist style. They held a joint exhibition in 1929, of which one reviewer wrote: 'If there are any associations connected with these patterns they belong to the category of mechanical designs.' Also related to Vorticism were some of the printed linens designed by Gregory Brown for Foxton's which were shown in Paris at the 1925 Exhibition.

Madeleine Kohn's bookbindings in abstract, geometrical designs owed much to the fact that she worked a lot of the time in Paris and was probably aware of Legrain's work. Serge Chermayeff, who lived in England from boyhood, was made director of Waring & Gillow's Modern Art Studio in 1928, and the foyer he designed for the Cambridge Theatre, London, demonstrated an assimilation of the Cubist geometrical style which had been avant-garde in Paris a few years before. Denham MacLaren was designing modern furniture made out of glass and tubular steel in the early 1930s which bears comparison with anything being produced on the Continent at the time.

By 1933 Wells Coates, an architect, was designing tubular steel furniture for PEL (Practical Equipment Ltd.—the name suggests an acquaintance with Le Corbusier's ideas). This was strongly influenced by Marcel Breuer's work, and two years later the German designer came to London in person, fleeing from the Nazi regime. During the time he was in England, Breuer worked as a consultant to the Isokon Furniture Company, for which he designed furniture made out of bent plywood. The technique had been pioneered in Scandinavia where designers such as Alvar Aalto and Bruno Mathsson had used it from the early 1930s.

Although the designers who created the 'modern' style were to a large extent reacting against the luxurious, decorated exhibits of the 1925 Exhibition in Paris, the work of Le Corbusier or Breuer was as characteristic of its era as an ensemble by Maurice Dufrène or a commode by Ruhlmann. Contemporaries might have contrasted a poster by Cassandre with a poster by Dupas, but today they are regarded as belonging to the same style—Deco.

To summarize, two distinct categories of modern art contributed to the Deco style. On the one hand, there was avant-garde architecture and design, which contemporaries called 'modernism'. It developed from Futurism, through De Stijl, Constructivism and the Bauhaus. Upheld by doctrinaire theory, it almost constituted a philosophy of life. To the Deco interior, it gave space and light. Whole walls were built in strengthened glass. Patterned wallpapers were abandoned. Artificial lighting tended to be almost theatrical. Built-in cupboards were favoured, and metal was used extensively in the construction of furniture.

On the other hand, Cubist painting of the Ecole de Paris contributed to the Deco style a new decorative vocabulary. In many instances the African art which had inspired the early Cubists was exploited by designers and decorators. Geometrical ornament, more or less abstract, appeared on carpets, glass, pottery, metalwork and jewellery. Intersecting squares, circles and triangles, chevrons and zigzags at first accompanied and then to a large extent supplanted the fawns and greyhounds, the tightly bunched flowers and the lissom figures which dominated the Paris Exhibition of 1925. With the Great Depression and the rise of Nazi Germany, European and American artists soon abandoned the more lyrical Art Deco of 'les Années Folles'.

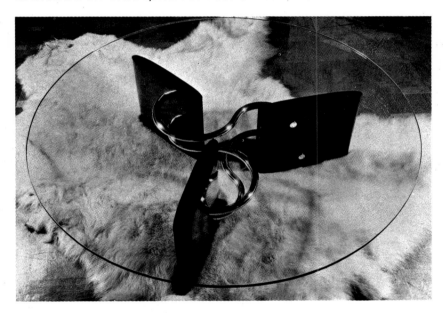

Table of glass and metal, by Denham MacLaren, 1931.

Above Original drawing for a
poster, around 1925, by
Charles Loupot. In this poster
Loupot employs some of the
graphic principles of
Futurism.

Below Original drawing for a poster, 1924, by Charles Loupot. During the twenties the motor-car and the aeroplane were idolized. Speed became an obsession, and artists sought the means to express it. Here Loupot chooses the horse as a symbol, and depicts it with distorted proportions and rippling mane — very much according to one set of Art Deco conventions.

Below Poster by Cassandre (Adolphe Mouron), around 1929. The style of several posters designed by Cassandre for travel companies reflects the art of the Italian Futurists, who declared speed to be one of the beauties of the modern age.

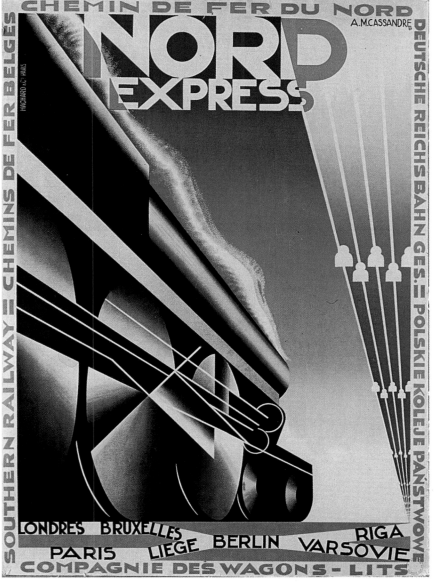

Right Chair, 1923, designed by Gerrit Rietveld for the Dutch pavilion at the 1923 Berlin Exhibition.

Opposite Red-blue chair designed by Gerrit Rietveld, around 1917. Although not a member of the De Stijl group until 1919, Rietveld made this chair according to De Stijl principles. Only black and primary colours are used and, apart from the plywood seat and back, the chair is constructed from vertical and horizontal members.

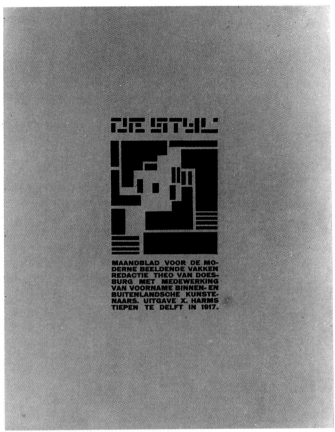

Above Cover of the first issue of *De Stijl* magazine designed by Theo van Doesburg, 1917. The original members of the De Stijl group, formed in neutral Holland during the First World War, included the painters Piet Mondrian, Bart van Leck and Theo van Doesburg, and the architects J.J.P. Oud and Jan Wils. The aim of the group was to create a language of form and colour applicable to every sphere of modern life.

Right Chair designed by Marcel Breuer, made at the Bauhaus, around 1923. Breuer joined the Bauhaus as a student in 1920, and was appointed head of the cabinet-making workshop in 1925. This chair shows how influenced he was by De Stijl.

Above Chair designed by Ludwig Mies van der Rohe at the Bauhaus, around 1929. Inspired by the example of Thonet's bentwood furniture of the nineteenth century, the Bauhaus pioneered the use of tubular steel. Later, metal was widely used by Deco designers.

Below 'Wassily' chair designed by Marcel Breuer at the Bauhaus, around 1926. Founded in 1919 by Walter Gropius, the Bauhaus first adhered to Expressionism; then, under the influence of van Doesburg, De Stijl ideas were assimilated, and, later, Laszlo Moholy-Nagy introduced Russian Constructivism to the school.

Above Bed-sitting-room
designed by Walter Gropius
and Marcel Breuer, 1927.
This is an example of the
Bauhaus style (although

Gropius denied its
existence), where the
furniture and fittings are as
homogeneous as they would
be in any Art Deco interior.

Above Coffee- and tea-service in silver with wooden handles designed by Marianne Brandt at the Bauhaus, around 1924. Marianne Brandt's designs are composed of geometrical elements in keeping with the Bauhaus dogma, but she instils into her metalwork a personal note of elegant curves and angles. Her style is an instance where it is impossible to make any distinction between 'modernist' and 'Art Deco'.

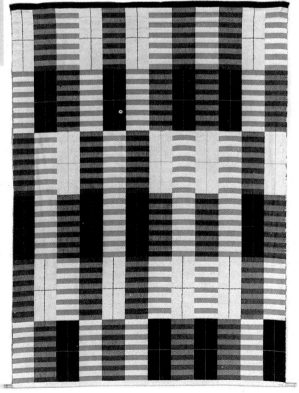

Below Wall-hanging woven by Anni Albers at the Bauhaus, 1926.

Left Sonia Delaunay's boutique on the Pont Alexandre III at the 1925 Paris Exhibition. Sonia Delaunay showed rugs, handbags and screens in the boutique, which she shared with the furrier Heim.

Above Watercolour drawings by Sonia Delaunay for fabrics. Neither as rigid nor as doctrinaire as the Bauhaus style, Sonia Delaunay's decorative designs have a similar appearance.

Right Carpet woven to a design by Sonia Delaunay, around 1930. Simultaneism was an abstract style developed from Cubism by Robert Delaunay, Sonia's husband.

Right Russian pavilion at the 1925 Paris Exhibition, designed by the architect Konstantin Melnikov. In this building, the most advanced at the Exhibition, Melnikov used the Constructivist style which had been developed in Russia by Vladimir Tatlin.

Below Teapot in porcelain decorated after a design by Chasnik. Just as Cubism was adapted to the decorative arts, so Suprematism, developed during the First World War by the painters Kasimir Malevich and El Lissitsky, was used in the years following the Russian Revolution to decorate everyday objects.

Left Pavillon du Tourisme at the 1925 Paris Exhibition, designed by Robert Mallet-Stevens. Inspired by the architectural sketches of the Italian Futurist Antonio Sant'Elia, Mallet-Stevens's pavilion was built in reinforced concrete. It was situated not far from the Grand Palais, to which it must have been a remarkable contrast.

Above Interior, Pavillon de l'Esprit Nouveau, designed by Le Corbusier for the 1925 Paris Exhibition. Le Corbusier filled the pavilion with office furniture and cheap, bentwood chairs by Thonet.

With the painter Amédée Ozenfant, he had introduced Purism, and paintings in this style are hanging on the wall.

Left Pavillon de l'Esprit Nouveau at the 1925 Paris Exhibition, designed by Le Corbusier. The Swiss-born architect had worked in Peter Behrens' office before the First World War, where he had learnt to use simple geometrical forms with large areas of fenestration. The Cubist sculpture on the lawn, by Jacques Lipchitz, indicates another influence on Le Corbusier.

Right: L'atelier de la modiste painted by Picasso in 1926. It was the interlocking and overlapping planes, organized on a framework of straight lines, of Cubist paintings such as this which spawned a distinct kind of Art Deco in Paris during the twenties.

Right The 'bar sous le toit', an interior designed by Charlotte Perriand and exhibited at the 1928 Salon d'Automne, from a contemporary illustration. On the strength of this design, Le Corbusier invited Charlotte Perriand to join his office.

Left Studio designed by Pierre Chareau, 1929, from a contemporary illustration. Chareau was one of those designers whose style progressed from traditional Art Deco to the modernist version.

Right Table and chairs in basket-work, a gouache drawing by Pierre Chareau, around 1930. Modernism in France employed to a large extent the traditional colour schemes of Art Deco.

Above Living-room designed
by René Herbst, 1925, from a
contemporary illustration.
Herbst, who was always
strongly opposed to
superfluous ornament, was a
founder-member of the
Union des Artistes Modernes
in 1930.

Above Nursery designed by
Francis Jourdain, 1925, from
a contemporary illustration.
'A room', wrote Jourdain,
'can be arranged very
luxuriously using less, rather
than more, furniture.'

Below **Sofa designed by Jules Leleu, around 1930. This piece illustrates how some French designers adapted rather than absorbed modernist ideas.**

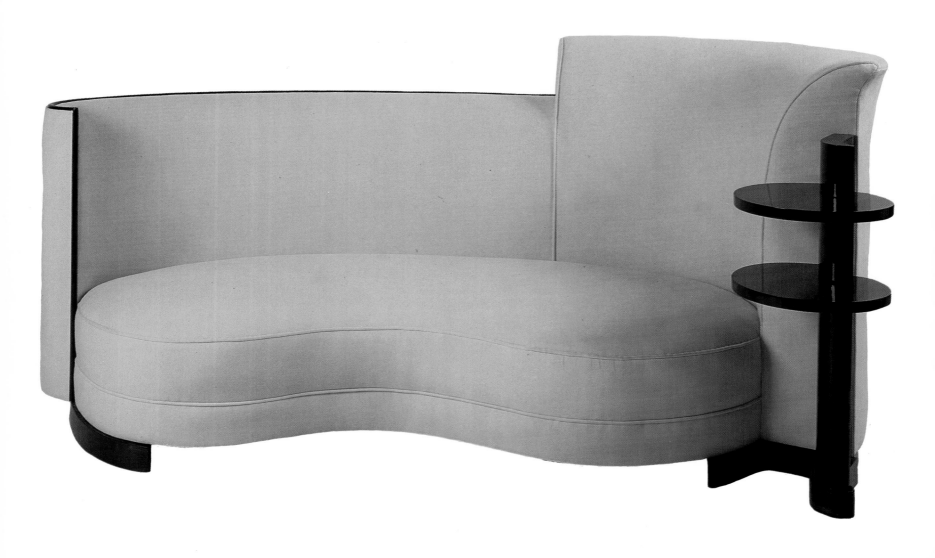

Left Dressing-table and stool in ash and aluminium designed by Süe et Mare, 1933. By the mid-thirties, even such traditionalists as Süe et Mare had compromised with the modernist style.

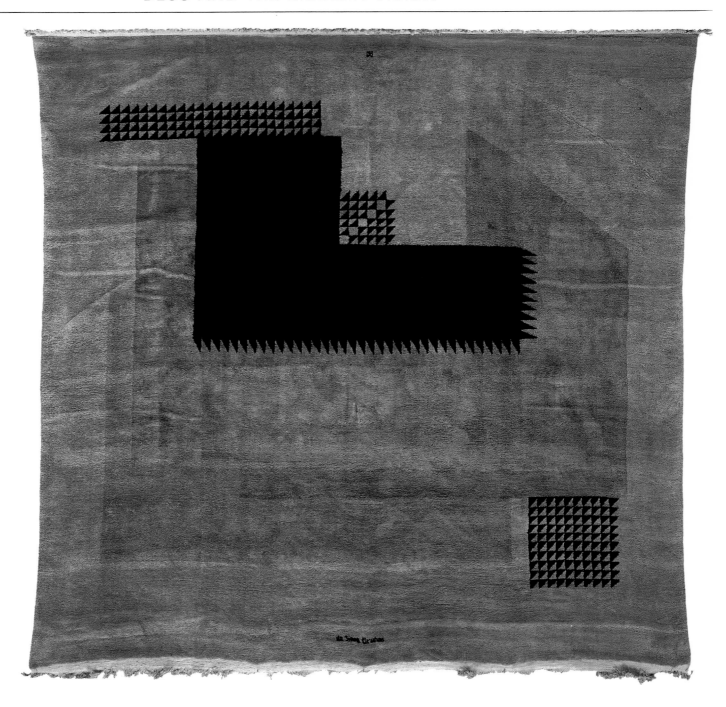

Right Hand-knotted carpet by
Bruno da Silva Bruhns,
around 1932. The design of
this carpet shows how
Bruhns progressed from
his earlier use of North
African motifs and the Greek
key-pattern.

Left Desk in macassar ebony with chrome-plated bronze handles, designed by Jacques-Emile Ruhlmann, around 1931. Chrome was widely used during the 1930s by designers who strove to meet the demands of modernist taste.

Right Armchair covered in shagreen designed by Jean Michel Frank, around 1928. Frank worked on a limited number of interiors for very wealthy clients, using luxurious materials in a restrained style.

Above Sideboard in wood with tubular steel and metal-wire handles, designed by René Herbst, around 1930. Herbst was one of the few French designers who always worked in an uncompromisingly modernist style.

Opposite Table in palisander wood and etched glass, and *(left)* standard lamp in painted sheet metal, both designed by Pierre Chareau around 1928. In these pieces Chareau declares his allegiance to the modernist style derived from Cubist painting and sculpture.

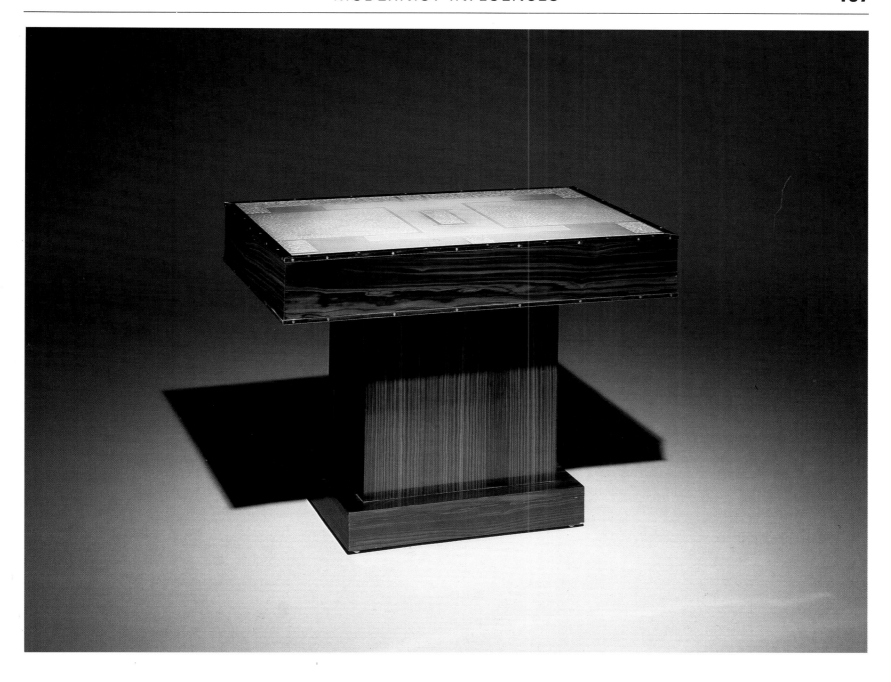

Right: Bureau-bibliothèque designed by Pierre Chareau for Jacques Doucet, around 1924. The desk, stool and chairs were designed by Pierre Legrain, the carpet by Louis Marcoussis. Doucet's collection of Cubist paintings inspired the designers and decorators who worked for him. Legrain developed an African style, reflecting the Cubists' interest in primitive art.

Below Chair of burr maple and shagreen designed by Pierre Legrain, around 1926. A very similar chair can be seen in the photograph opposite of Doucet's *bureau-bibliothèque.*

Above Table covered in shagreen designed around 1925 by Marcel Coard, another artist who was patronized by Jacques Doucet.

Above **Salon of the Roquebrune villa which Eileen Gray, in collaboration with Jean Badovici, built for herself in the late 1920s.**

Right Seat designed by Eileen Gray, 1925. Having studied at the Slade School in London, Eileen Gray settled in Paris in 1907. There she started her own workshops and opened a boutique where her furniture and rugs were on sale. The couturier Jacques Doucet was among her earliest clients.

Left Sofa designed by Eileen Gray for the Suzanne Talbot apartment in 1924.

Jean Dunand worked first as a sculptor before he turned to metalwork. His interest in patination led to his use of lacquer, the technique of which he learnt in 1912. During the twenties and thirties he made furniture and metalwork, progressing from a figurative to a geometrical style, inspired from time to time by African themes. All the pieces shown here and on the following pages date from around 1920 to 1935.

Right Cigarette-box decorated with red, black and gold lacquer, by Jean Dunand.

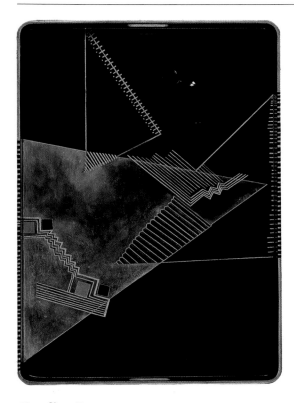

Above Cigarette-case
decorated with red and black
lacquer, by Jean Dunand.

Opposite Bookshelves
covered with red lacquer, by
Jean Dunand.

Right Vase decorated with
red and black lacquer, by
Jean Dunand. The pedestal,
in ebony, was designed by
Clément Rousseau.

Left Vase decorated with black and red lacquer and crushed eggshell, by Jean Dunand.

Below Vase decorated with red and black lacquer, by Jean Dunand.

Left Vase decorated with red,
black and gold lacquer, by
Jean Dunand.

Left Vase decorated with red,
black and gold lacquer, by
Jean Dunand.

Below Vase decorated with
red and black lacquer, by
Jean Dunand.

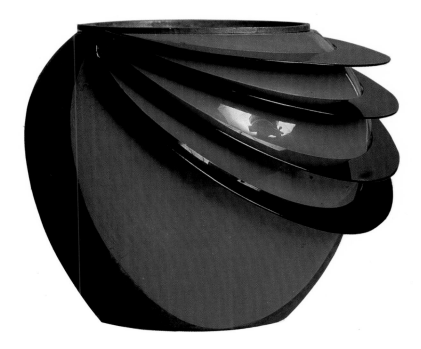

Right Glass jar and cover by Maurice Marinot, around 1925. A painter who turned to the decoration of glass in 1911, Marinot became increasingly concerned with the decorative potential of the material itself. In 1922 he stopped painting his glassware with figurative designs in enamels and turned to acid-etched geometrical motifs, self-coloured glass, and the decorative exploitation of defects in the material.

Below Glass bottle by
Maurice Marinot, 1920s.

Left Glass vase with acid-
etched decoration, by
Maurice Marinot, around
1924.

Above Glass bottles by
Maurice Marinot, around
1930.

Left Tea-set by Jean Puiforcat, around 1930. A founder-member of the Union des Artistes Modernes, Puiforcat, too, adopted a modernist style. The forms of his silverware are derived from Cubism.

Right Clock by Jean Puiforcat, around 1930. Puiforcat's remarkably imaginative use of the simplest elements is well demonstrated here.

Above Stoneware vase by Emile Decœur, around 1930. Having abandoned the floral decoration of his pre-1925 pottery, Decœur concentrated on simple shapes and glaze effects.

Left Coloured glass vase, with acid-etched decoration, by Daum, around 1930. The Nancy glass factory adopted this modernist style following the success of Marinot and other individual craftsmen.

Right Necklace in coral, onyx, jade and diamonds by Georges Fouquet, around 1925. These materials are typical of Georges Fouquet's work from 1922, when he abandoned traditional jewellery.

Right Design for a pendant by the architect Eric Bagge for Georges Fouquet, around 1929. Other artists who worked for Fouquet included the painter André Léveillé, the poster designer Cassandre and the sculptor Jean Lambert-Rucki.

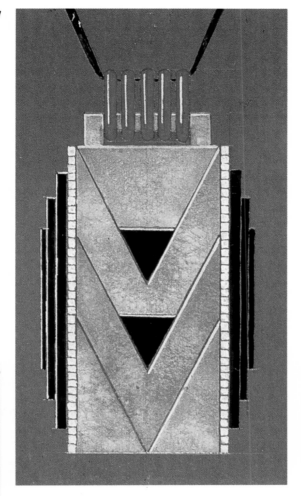

Below Brooch in platinum, coral, jade and diamonds designed by Gérard Sandoz, around 1928. The nephew of Paul Follot, Sandoz was a painter and poster artist as well as a jewellery designer.

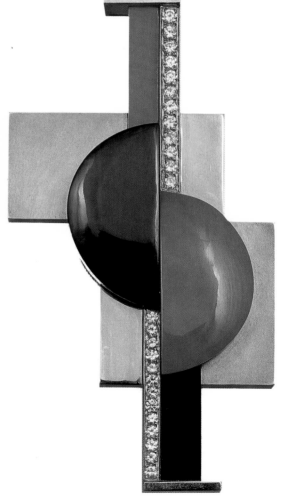

Above Brooch in silver, diamonds and enamels by Raymond Templier, 1929. Templier, a founder member of the Union des Artistes Modernes, made jewellery and cigarette-cases. The latter were sometimes decorated in enamels with sporting subjects; otherwise Templier worked in an austere, geometrical style.

Above Cigarette-box in
silver, decorated with
enamels, by Jean Goulden,
around 1927. Having pursued
a medical career up to the
end of the First World War,
Goulden became fascinated
by Byzantine enamels while
visiting the monastery at
Mount Athos on his way
home from the Macedonian
front. Returning to France, he
learnt from Jean Dunand the
technique of champlevé
enamels, and started his own
workshop, producing work in
a modernist style.

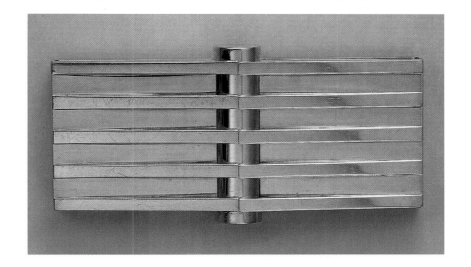

Above Gold vanity case by
Jean Fouquet, around 1928.
Joining his father's firm in
1919, Jean Fouquet was
influenced by Le Corbusier.
With his father, he worked in
a modernist manner from
1922, often designing pieces
of jewellery in Cubist or
African styles.

Left Lamp in silver, decorated
with enamels, by Jean
Goulden, around 1928.

Above Design sketch for the foyer of the Cambridge Theatre, London, by Serge Chermayeff, around 1930. The architect and designer Chermayeff ran Waring & Gillow's modern French furniture department from 1929. The relaxed modernism of his style shows an affinity with the work of the U.A.M. designers in France.

Below Dressing-table by Betty Joel Ltd., around 1930. Betty Joel and her husband David founded their furniture company at the end of the First World War. They designed simple, functional pieces for small houses, and, as this dressing-table indicates, developed a sophisticated geometrical style.

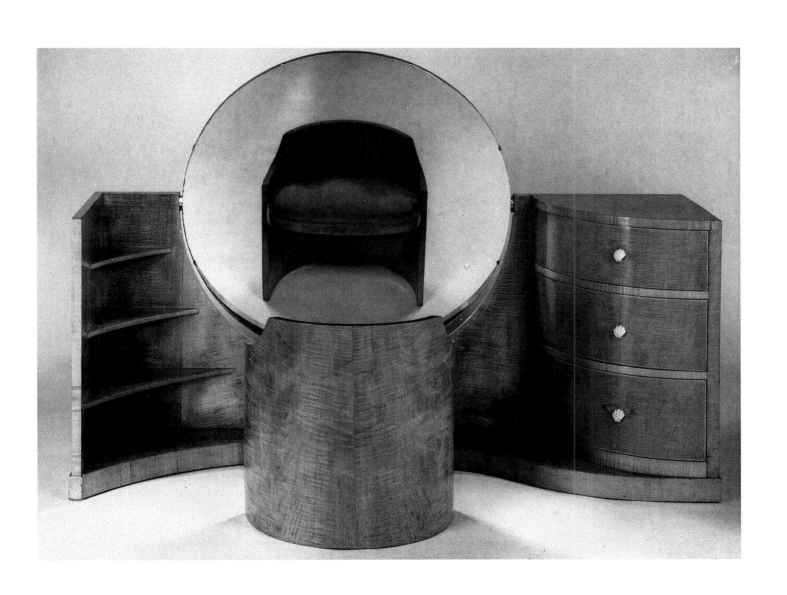

Right Cupboard doors in marquetry designed by Roger Fry for the Omega Workshops, around 1914. By organizing exhibitions of modern continental painting in London, Fry introduced Cubism to the British public. He was one of the first artists to adapt the style to the applied arts.

Left Box in silver and ivory by Charles Boyton, around 1930. Boyton's work is representative of a small group of English silversmiths who, towards the end of the twenties, broke away from the Arts and Crafts manner.

Left Linen designed by Gregory Brown for Foxton's, around 1925. Vorticism, a style loosely based on Futurism, was generally abandoned by English painters and sculptors during the years immediately following the First World War. But it was preserved through the twenties in the work of a few designers, including Edward McKnight Kauffer and Gregory Brown.

'The only reason why America was not represented at the Exhibition of Decorative Industrial Art in Paris in 1925 was because we found that we had no decorative art. Not only was there a sad lack of achievement that could be exhibited but we discovered that there was not even a serious movement in this direction and that the general public was quite unconscious of the fact that modern art had been extended into the field of business and industry. On the other hand we had our skyscrapers and at that very date they had been developed to such an extent that, if it had been possible to have sent an entire building abroad, it would have been a more vital contribution in the field of modern art than all the things done in Europe added together.' (Paul Frankl, 1928)

This statement by Frankl illustrates the peculiar nature of American design in the first two decades of this century. America was certainly a fertile source of Deco imagery: American jazz and the presence in Europe of black musicians and dancers contributed to the popular interest in Negro art and culture; the ancient ethnic arts of the Americas, the Inca and Mayan cultures, were plundered for their design motifs; and, perhaps more importantly, the whole mood of America after the First World War—its newness, its prosperity, and its rapidly growing cities and industries—represented the spirit of the new century. By 1920 America was in advance of Europe in its technology, particularly in those areas which had a direct bearing on architecture and interior design. Electric lighting was pioneered in the States, as was central heating and automatic rubbish disposal, and the first building to incorporate steel as a structural element was the New York Home Insurance Company office, built in Chicago by Jenney in 1885. So, in theory, America was the perfect arena for the new styles of modernism and Deco. Yet they were slower to take root there than anywhere else in the western world. It was only when the language of Deco was transformed into something more purely American that it spread and developed, becoming by the end of the thirties the first unified American design movement.

At the beginning of the century, America was still a relatively new nation; there were dozens of different cultures, a large range of vernacular design, and a world of difference between the architecture of the big cities and that of the small provincial towns. In design, there was little that was recognizably American. The upper and middle classes were strongly conservative in their taste, preferring reproduction colonial and continental furniture to anything 'modern', and while the general public was quite ready to accept modernism where appropriate, in the design of the automobile for instance, where it impinged on domestic life the resistance was considerable and there was still a tendency to dress technological advance in old clothes—the phonograph, for example, was disguised as a chest, tallboy or buffet.

The exceptions to the conservative and derivative nature of design in America lay in the work of Louis Comfort Tiffany, the Arts and Crafts

Phonograph, Shear Maddox Furniture Company, 1925. This phonograph is disguised as a Renaissance cabinet, the only clue to its real identity being the handle protruding from its side.

Vase of silver, turquoise and beaten copper, Tiffany & Co., 1900. This vase shows the influence of American Indian design on the Arts and Crafts movement in the United States. The overall shape and surface decoration derive from traditional basket weaving, but despite this vernacular quality, it remains a costly and sophisticated object.

movement and Frank Lloyd Wright, all heavily influenced by new movements in European design. The Arts and Crafts movement in America exerted a considerable influence on upper- and middle-class taste in the early years of the century, but it too was put at the service of revivalism, with Stickley of Fayetteville, for example, advertising 'reproductions from the most picturesque period of American home life'. Only Frank Lloyd Wright, a leading figure in the movement, succeeded in transforming the English Arts and Crafts philosophy into something distinctly American, notably in his Prairie houses.

In the twenties, however, interest in contemporary European design gradually gathered impetus. European furniture became available in exclusive shops, and wealthy Americans, recognizing Paris as the fashion capital of the world, bought French Deco furniture and flocked to the couture houses. The Vienna Secession, too, enjoyed a period of popularity that lasted well into the twenties, with Edward Aschermann of the Aschermann studios as one of its major exponents. The true significance of the new European design, though, seems to have been largely ignored, except by Frank Lloyd Wright, and when in 1926 selected exhibits from the 1925 Paris Exhibition were shown in the Metropolitan Museum and elsewhere, they were ill received. The design magazines questioned the comfort of the pieces and cautioned against 'novelty for novelty's sake'; some writers felt that this European design was not suitable for America (Sarah M. Lockwood, for example, in 'Let's Go Slow about this Modernist Movement', *Country Life*, 1929); and there was little response from manufacturers, who were unwilling to invest money in what appeared to be a passing fad.

To stimulate a reaction from industry, Macy's department store staged, in 1928, the first 'International Exposition of Art in Industry' and the following year the Metropolitan Museum presented 'The Architect and the Industrial Arts', with thirteen room settings by prominent designers, including Raymond Hood, Eliel Saarinen and Joseph Urban. The latter exhibition emphasized the value of integrating the room and its furnishings, a concept dear to Art Deco designers and also to Frank Lloyd Wright, but the displays had little to do with mass production and industry as most of the furniture was handmade from expensive materials.

The real impetus to the development of modernism and Deco in America came with the immigration to the States of European designers, among them Joseph Urban, Eugene Schoen, Kem Weber and Eliel Saarinen. Their ideas, firmly based on European modernism, exerted a strong influence on young designers in America, many of whom had also visited Europe. Conversely, America exerted a great influence on them—not American design, but the nature of American life and industry—and it is this amalgamation that gives Deco in the States its particular flavour.

An important repository of European ideals was the Cranbrook Academy of Art near Detroit, an artistic community and art and design school under the direction of Eliel Saarinen, an architect who had come to America from his native Finland in 1922. He designed both the building and its furnishings, and his awareness of unified design is particularly evident in his own quarters, where he and his wife Loja conceived every detail of the interior, including the ceramics and light-fittings. As a fusion of two traditions, the modernist and the Arts and Crafts, Cranbrook may be seen in the same light as the Macy's and Metropolitan exhibitions, and its influence continued throughout the twenties and thirties. The European immigrant Paul Frankl was another enthusiastic champion of the Modern Movement and articles by him appeared regularly throughout the second half of the twenties, with titles such as 'Form and Re-form'. But although Frankl was a propagandist for non-referential design, he still produced furniture in the continental style in the twenties, simply because his fashionable clientele preferred European Deco.

The supreme achievement of American design at the time of the 1925 Paris Exhibition was, as Frankl rightly observed, the skyscraper. It was an architectural form developed from necessity, a means of coping with the restricted urban space in cities such as New York. But it surpassed that necessity to become a satisfying symbol of commercial and urban power and, on a more fanciful level, of man's refusal to accept the mundane laws of gravity. This symbolic value is demonstrated by the speed at which the skyscraper was adopted in cities and towns where space was no particular problem. The typical stepped shape can be traced to an equally mundane source: the 1916 New York City zoning ordinance which stated that all tall buildings should be set back in stages to allow light into the street. This stepped shape swiftly transcended its origins to become the ziggurat, which in turn became an integral part of the language of Deco.

Despite the radical nature of the skyscraper and the technology involved in its construction, the decorative language most frequently used by builders before the mid-twenties was Gothic, in many ways the natural style for such strongly vertical structures. Architects, such as Cass Gilbert in the Woolworth Building (see page 00), used Gothic ornament in an inventive and visually exciting way which influenced skyscraper design for over a decade.

The two Americans most responsible for the transition from eclecticism were Raymond Hood and Hugh Ferriss, the former essentially a theorist, the latter a prolific architect. In his book *The Metropolis of Tomorrow* (1929) Ferriss envisioned a city of gigantic buildings, each designed according to its function. The towers of the 'Science Zone', for example, are quartz-crystal-like structures with, he said, 'no Gothic branch, no acanthus leaf, no recollection of the plant world'. Hood, with his partner John Mead Howells, won a competition in 1922 to design the Chicago Tribune Tower. Their design was for a highly decorated Gothic tower; that it should have been selected in preference to Eliel Saarinen's more simple and virtually unornamented entry is not surprising, and Gropius's entirely modernist structure was not even placed. In his subsequent work, culminating in the Rockefeller Center,

Hood's skyscrapers became progressively simplified, with less historical ornament and more emphasis on the archetypal stepped silhouette and soaring central tower. The Rockefeller Center, begun in 1931, is perhaps the best example of this style and it certainly dictated the design of skyscrapers in New York for almost a decade. As befits New York's aspirations in the late twenties to be the home of new culture, the Center is a complex of offices, theatres, shops and restaurants, including the R.K.O. Roxy and the Radio City Music Hall.

The Empire State Building of 1932 by Shreve, Lamb & Harmon shows the same monumental scale—102 storeys—as the Rockefeller Center. With its mast for mooring airships, it was intended to be a monument to the future, but unfortunately the powerful updraughts created by the canyons of tall buildings made the use of airships totally impractical in cities. The building demonstrates one of the flaws inherent in monumental skyscraper design: the vast structure depends on internal services such as elevators, yet these take up so much space that much of the function of the structure—to make use of limited ground area—is lost.

In contrast to this simplified and monumental aspect of Deco, the 1930 Chrysler Building by William Van Alen is a supreme example of a more flamboyant Deco, illustrating perfectly the complex nature of these structures. The overall shape is a ziggurat surmounted by a tower and spire, and the sculpted decoration consists of automobile motifs, hub-caps, radiators, mud-guards and fins. The building functions as a complete image of the Chrysler Corporation, suggesting both the Chrysler product and the enormous financial power of the company. Van Alen accomplished this with a light touch and the building, for all its symbolism, is not didactic, but simply glamorous. The exterior glistens and the disciplined vertical bands of the windows lead to the flamboyant 'crown' of the tower. Valid comparisons are to be made not just with architecture but with dress, and the Chrysler Building owes much to movie costume—the clothes designed by Travis Banton for De Mille's *Cleopatra* in the early thirties for example. Like the best movie costume, the Chrysler Building borrows quite freely from various historical languages without any need for period accuracy. Van Alen was not reconstructing the past or making a pastiche of an Egyptian temple, a Byzantine basilica or the Hanging Gardens of Babylon, although elements of all these might be found in the Chrysler Building; Banton was not seriously reconstructing Egyptian costume. Instead, both men in their own disciplines were making something new, full of witty and deliberate historical references.

The interior decoration of skyscrapers was as important as the exterior, for most of them were public buildings in one sense or another. The Rockefeller Center was, of course, a truly public building, but even company skyscrapers were used by hordes of office workers and visitors. In the lobbies of buildings like the Chrysler, the Chanin and the R.K.O. Roxy the motifs and forms of the exterior were echoed and elaborated in radiator grilles, elevator doors, light-fittings and mural

Claudette Colbert as Cleopatra, 1934.

decorations. New technology in the shape of elevators, central heating apparatus and light-fittings gave designers like Deskey, W. Wyatt Hibbs, Saarinen and Schoen the opportunity to design virtually new objects. The interiors of skyscrapers often represent real design collaboration and some of the most innovative textiles of the twenties were designed within this discipline.

In America it was the architects who led the development of the new Deco style—unlike in Europe, where the artistic vanguard was to be found in the world of fashion. Some American designers had first trained as architects and, like Eliel Saarinen, were known first in the States for their buildings. Also, many designers of furniture and decorative items turned for inspiration to architecture, particularly the powerful and complex images of skyscrapers. Paul Frankl, for example, produced a line of furniture between 1925 and 1930 which he called 'Skyscraper'. Here maple, plastics and metallic finishes were used on pieces which were directly related in their shapes to the stepped-back lines of contemporary skyscrapers. Frankl believed that interiors should relate to their external surroundings and his furniture literally brought the shapes of the newly constructed New York skyline into the urban apartment. Many of his pieces were multi-functional units which combined cupboards, display units and bookcases. Here the influence of architecture was practical as well as functional, for many urban apartments were fairly small and such furniture was not only fashionably modern but also necessary.

The architectural language of Deco was not confined to the cities or to skyscrapers and it is interesting to compare a commercial temple like the Chrysler Building with a church of the same period, for instance Bruce Goff's Boston Avenue Methodist church from Tulsa. Goff used the same basic format of a stepped tower surmounting, in this case, a pinnacled block. The combination of block and tower might at first glance be Gothic, but the effect is completely Deco, powerfully optimistic and very worldly. That Goff's church should have been built in Tulsa at all indicates how rapidly the skyscraper spread through the States from the mid-twenties. One would expect to find such a structure in Chicago or Pittsburgh, but Tulsa was a spacious new city, the wealth of which was derived from oil, and the visual evidence of this civic wealth was expressed naturally in the skyscraper.

In the domestic sphere, Frank Lloyd Wright, whose work in the first two decades of the century had shown a powerful understanding of modernism, was producing private residences before the twenties which reflected the preoccupations of Deco translated into the American idiom. The Barnsdall (Hollyhock) house built in Los Angeles in 1917 is in many ways the prototype of Californian Deco. It is based on Mayan architecture and incorporates decorative elements on the exterior derived from pylons; these punctuate both the skyline and the white surfaces of the articulated blocks which make up the house. The house is monumental, without rising at any point beyond two storeys in height. Just as the skyscrapers work within their environment in the cities, the Hollyhock house works within the landscape; it too is expressive of power but, unlike the essentially public skyscrapers, it guards and protects its interior space. Lloyd Wright did not copy Mayan architecture for the Hollyhock house any more than Van Alen copied any historical style for the Chrysler Building. Twenties Deco is, at its best, able to move from style to style, taking what it needs from each in the service of something new.

This interest in ancient cultures, such a fertile source of Deco imagery, was largely stimulated by the discovery in 1922 of Tutankhamun's tomb. Egyptian themes became highly popular, as did those of the early American cultures. Wright was one of the first designers to make use of Mayan forms, but the publication in 1928 of Franz Boa's book *Primitive Arts* revealed the real richness of the ancient cultures of the Americas to a wide range of designers. Patterns relating to Aztec and Inca motifs appear in the work of several American potters, notably Maija Grotel, who taught at Cranbrook, Dorothea Warren O'Hara and Maria Martinez. The same repertoire of geometricized natural forms appears in the textiles produced by Loja Saarinen and her studio.

A second phase in the development of Deco in America was initiated, ironically, by the Depression, during which the style was spread and popularized throughout the country and finally appeared in mass-produced objects. In architecture the richly decorated style of the twenties was too expensive and, in any case, inappropriate to the mood of the thirties; but the basic forms of Deco were so adaptable that they became virtually the official style for buildings produced under the Public Works Administration and the Works Progress Administration. Set up as part of Franklin D. Roosevelt's New Deal to provide work for architects, designers, builders and decorative artists, the PWA and the WPA sponsored public building across the nation in the shape of schools, libraries, courthouses and so on. The monuments of this second phase clearly show the influence of European modernism. Behrens' work, particularly, was admired by architects like Bertram Goodhue who designed the Nebraska State Capitol in Lincoln.

The collaboration between architect, designer, sculptor and painter, which had been so fruitful in the twenties, was continued in the following decade. All the buildings constructed under the aegis of the PWA/WPA were intended to be decorated, not in the opulent fashion of skyscrapers but with sculptures and paintings appropriate to the function of the building. The slightly playful, fantasy symbolism of the Chrysler Building was replaced by a more serious didactic system, with much of the decoration concentrating on American themes.

The greatest stylistic innovation of the Depression era was that of 'streamlining'. This was partially the product of the great wave of European designers who fled to the States from fascism and the imminent war. The Bauhaus was closed in 1933 and Gropius, van der Rohe, Josef Albers and Laszlo Moholy-Nagy all emigrated to America, bringing with them Bauhaus theories and the philosophy of functionalism. These ideas were already known in the States and had been translated with some caution by Frankl, Donald Deskey and others, but in the Depression they were seen as a solution to economic problems and, in combination with ideas that came directly from industry and commerce, they generated streamlining.

Streamlining was not exclusively an American idea—it had been discussed by the Futurists in Italy before the First World War—but what had been merely a theory to the Futurists could be a reality in post-war America, which had the technology and the manufacturing processes to realize the streamlined train, the streamlined automobile and even streamlined architecture. One of the prophets of streamlining in America was Norman Bel Geddes, an industrial designer who came into the field from the theatre and advertising (he worked as a freelance for J. Walter Thompson). Interestingly, the two other pioneers of the style, Walter Dorwin Teague and Raymond Loewy, had also worked in advertising. Many of Bel Geddes's ideas were visionary rather than practical, but he was instrumental in gaining recognition for industrial design in the thirties and in breaking down the barriers which existed between industrial design and architecture. By the mid-thirties streamlining was an accepted language for building; more than that, it was seen as a symbol of optimism and promise for the future. In 1934 Egmont Arens proposed to Roosevelt that streamlining should be adopted officially as a symbol for the restructuring of the American economy, and the World Fair Exposition of 1939 became a public demonstration of this patriotic confidence.

In architecture streamlining was the perfect language for commerce, although it made little impact on domestic building. Unlike the lavish and ultimately expensive first phase of Deco, the nature of streamlining enabled it to work at every economic level, from the factories of the commercial giants like the Coca-Cola company to small gas stations, diners and bars. The materials from which streamlined architecture was constructed were modern—baked enamel panels, plastics, aluminium and so on—and their very modernity allowed them to be used on 'status' buildings despite the fact that they were also inexpensive. Conversely, their cheapness also made them available to small businesses. Streamlined buildings, too, could be prefabricated and the component parts used to 'dress up' existing structures. The appeal of streamlining is obvious, and in the second half of the thirties the style represented everything that was modern, efficient and clean. By the early forties it had become the most universal of the Deco sub-styles and later it was to be the most imitated in Deco revivals.

It was Frank Lloyd Wright who produced the most solid monuments of streamlining. One, the Guggenheim Museum in New York, was not actually built until 1959, fifteen years after it had been designed; the other, the Johnson Wax Building in Racine, Wisconsin, was designed as an overall concept with everything from the furniture to the light-fittings following the same dynamic curving line. This late phase of Lloyd Wright's work has been subject to much criticism, and the Johnson Wax Building particularly has been seen as an aberration bordering on the kitsch. In fact, it fits into the pattern of both Lloyd Wright's own work, with its history of unified design, and the prevailing mood of America at the end of the thirties.

The Depression was the same catalyst for furniture and interior design as it had been for architecture. During the twenties many designers had used machine art and mass-produced materials as a decorative motif in their work. Frankl's use of bakelite on his skyscraper furniture can be seen as an example of this, and Donald Deskey, too, translated the strict utilitarianism of the Bauhaus into something more playful and luxurious in his designs for Radio City. After the collapse of the New York stock market, however, the ensuing economic depression led the more versatile of American designers to consider seriously the possibilities of mass production. The 'machine style', which had been practised from choice by Deskey, Kem Weber and others, became the most appropriate style for mass production and the necessary use of cheaper materials. The 1934 Metropolitan Museum exhibition 'Contemporary American Industrial Art' was realistic in a way which the earlier 'The Architect and the Industrial Arts' was not. The settings showed a real relationship between the designer and industry in two ways: much of the furniture was constructed from industrial materials—metal, glass and plastics—and the overall design of the pieces indicated an awareness of the machine. Deskey, Kem Weber, Russel Wright, Gilbert Rohde and others espoused mass production and designed for companies like the hugely successful Herman Miller Company. Manufacturers who had initially held back from producing Deco were now able to see its commercial possibilities and were prepared to commit money to its production.

By the mid-thirties it becomes difficult to find a clear dividing line between industrial design and interior or furniture design. The products of industry were finding their way into the domestic interior, not simply into the kitchen but also into the dining-room and lounge. The radio and, later in the decade, the television, the telephone and the phonograph are examples of this invasion. Paradoxically, the Depression saw a boom in consumer goods; it was, in effect, a buyer's market and every effort was made to encourage the public to acquire, on the 'buy now, pay later' plan, the goods being turned out by such companies as Sears, General Electric and Eastman Kodak.

The ideas promoted by Bel Geddes found direct expression in the design of large-scale objects, such as trains and cars, the utilitarian interiors of kitchens, offices and hospitals, and in small consumer objects. These in turn exerted an influence on the overall appearance of domestic interiors to the extent that by the mid-thirties streamlining was an acceptable style for interior decoration, an interesting reversal of the situation at the beginning of the twenties when technology in the interior had been disguised. Only eleven years separate the Shear Maddox phonograph and the Walter Dorwin Teague radio of 1936, and the difference is not simply due to an advance in technology; it shows a clear shift in public attitudes towards that technology. Plastics, for example, had been used since before the turn of the century, but for the most part in 'acceptable' places, in automobiles and other new items. When used by designers they tended to be combined with fine materials, so demonstrating that they were being used for reasons of style not necessity. In the thirties, by contrast, plastics were being used for their own unique qualities—their bright colours, the versatility of their moulded and cast forms—which no other material had. A full discussion of plastics belongs more properly to the chapter on mass production, but they proved eminently suited to the language of streamlining and were used in a wide range of consumer items from furniture to novelties.

It would be wrong to suppose that streamlining was the only development of the Deco style in America during the thirties. The conservatism discussed earlier in this chapter still existed on every social level and was responsible for much low-standard, mass-produced 'traditional' furniture, but at the other end of the financial scale traditionalism and Deco fused with some interesting results.

This blend of historicism with modernism had its origins in England and France, where interior designers like Syrie Maugham were working with theatrical mixtures of genuine period furniture and objects and modern pieces, made either in imitation of the old or to blend with them. Syrie Maugham's own drawing-room of 1933 was particularly influential and received much publicity on both sides of the Atlantic for its colour scheme of white on white. This witty and elegant style became very popular in the States among both the established and the new rich, particularly in Hollywood. It flattered the owner with its implied knowledge of historical style, even if the actual decorative scheme had been devised by someone else—literally an interior designer like the hugely successful Elsie de Wolfe. It encompassed in a very satisfying way both the modern and the old and cherished. In 1946 Ralph Linton, professor of Anthropology at Yale University, wrote: 'As a reaction to the plenty of the machine came a desire for the unique object, for a one-of-a-kind, I-have-the-only-one piece. Master Alger and his boss have become a nation of antique lovers, another form of ancestor worship. Antiques established the appearance of long established social and family background, the desired effect of unearned increment.'

The best exponent of the style in America was probably J.H. Robsjohn-Gibbings who came from England in 1929 to work for Joseph Duveen, whose firm specialized in importing real antique pieces and in period reconstruction. In his book *Goodbye Mr Chippendale* Robsjohn-Gibbings describes his disgust with this unimaginative consumption of history. His own work drew on Ancient Greece for its inspiration, and in 1936 his showroom was set out with a mosaic floor and terracotta reliefs, furnished with modern pieces of his own design based on Greek prototypes. He decorated his schemes with a very few, carefully selected pieces of antique Classical sculpture or ceramics. The result was much more restrained than the mainstream Neo-Regency Mod-

Mae West on the set of *The Heat's On*, a Cecil B. De Mille film of 1943. The rococo-esque mirror and furniture, the rug and the pastel colouring of the room are all derived from Elsie de Wolfe, but the exaggeration of scale and the lush effect of the interior are pure Hollywood.

erne or Classical Moderne as practised by Duveen and others, although it still retains a slightly theatrical quality.

Robsjohn-Gibbings, Elsie de Wolfe, Duveen and other exponents of historical chic were also perhaps the greatest influence on design in the movies in the thirties. The work of Van Nest Polglase for the Astaire/Rogers films reflects the work of both Robsjohn-Gibbings and Elsie de Wolfe, exaggerating it until the theatrical element in their work becomes utterly theatrical.

The movies were, in fact, one of the gathering places for Deco in more ways than one. The films themselves drew ideas from fashion, interior design and architecture, glamourized them and then passed them on to their huge audiences. Costume designers like Adrian, and most particularly Travis Banton, drew with great fluency on every historical period to create costumes which are unmistakably Deco. Many mainstream professional designers also worked in Hollywood in the late twenties and early thirties; Kem Weber, Joseph Urban and Ely Jacques Kahn all designed for films. Urban expressed his feelings about the industry as early as 1920 when he wrote: 'The motion picture offers incomparably the greatest field to any creative artist of the brush or blueprint today. It is the art of the twentieth century and perhaps the greatest art of modern times. It is all so young, so fresh, so untried. It is like an unknown ocean stretching out before a modern Columbus.' Couturiers like Chanel, Maggy Rouff and Hermès all designed or provided clothes for films. Their ideas were dispersed among the mass public and often the cheapest products of Deco—mass-produced 'Five and Dime' Deco—are imitations of movie styles.

The movie theatres themselves are perhaps the most extravagant examples of the Deco style. The skyscraper style of the twenties, with its extravagant ornamentation and abundant references, carried on throughout the thirties, taking streamlining in its stride but still presenting the public with an environment of unimaginable opulence and glamour. The sheer size of many of these buildings, constructed when the cinema could count on a huge audience, made possible the mingling of styles as disparate as Egyptian and Spanish without inducing claustrophobia. These movie palaces are neither vulgar nor kitsch, and like all the best of American Deco they have a symbolic function: they are about the movies, they are for the movies, and they exist for a public that wanted an escape from the reality of the Depression. In a sense, they are also truly democratic, for anyone could go, providing they had the money for a ticket, and all this opulence was available for public consumption.

The great success of Deco in America lies in its adaptability on every level. It could, and did, become a truly popular style in the thirties because within the basic language of the style there was sufficient flexibility to make the transition between the Radio City Music Hall, a Cord 'Phaeton' car, a set piece for a Busby Berkeley film, a juke-box or the Louisiana State Capitol. This same flexibility made it appropriate for the exclusive or the mass-produced without ever losing its identity.

Right 'Man's Den' designed
by Joseph Urban for the
Metropolitan Museum
exhibition 'The Architect and
the Industrial Arts', 1929. The
exhibition was devoted to
American design and
manufacture, but this room
and others similar provoked
hostile reactions. In *Forum* a
critic wrote, 'This eccentric
trash will appeal to the
fiendish and excitable
Americans who maintain
homes but do not inhabit
them and who rush hither
and thither in search of
vicious amusements and
shocking adventures.'

Above Interior, the Robie house, Chicago, by Frank Lloyd Wright, 1908. In Wright's Prairie houses the interiors, including the furniture, were conceived as complete design units. He followed the unified design principles of the Arts and Crafts movement, but also believed in machine production and new technology. It is significant that in the Robie house even the electric lighting is seen as an integral part of the interior.

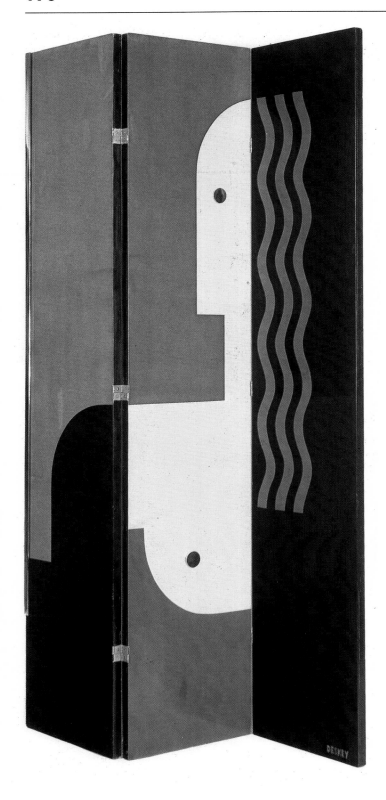

Left Screen for Gilbert Seldes, designed by Donald Deskey, 1931. In common with many young American designers in the thirties, Deskey looked to Europe for inspiration. This screen is obviously derived from the paintings of Fernand Léger, who in turn was inspired by the vitality of America.

Above Dressing-table, stool and mirror by Paul Frankl, 1930s. Though French influences are evident in the patterning of the mirror and glass panels of the dressing-table, this furniture, with its swing drawers and compact shape, responds to the requirements of American apartment living.

Right Side Chairs designed by Eliel Saarinen for his residence at Cranbrook, 1929–30. These chairs are in complete harmony with the overall decoration of the interior, which can be seen overleaf.

Above Living-room of the
Saarinen house, Cranbrook
Academy, 1928–30. Eliel
Saarinen was the first
director of the academy and
his own house demonstrates
perfectly his belief in unified
design. The furniture,
textiles, light fittings and
ceramic tiles of the fireplace
all share the same simplified
shapes, enriched by the
careful use of veneer, colour
and texture.

Above Orpheus Fountain at the Cranbrook Academy, by Carl Milles, 1938. Cranbrook was both a school of design and an artists' community. The fountain, which incorporates a sculptural group, demonstrates the importance of sculpture to Deco architecture. It also symbolically integrates the fine and decorative arts.

Above Entrance sculpture, Rockefeller Center, *Wisdom* by Lee Lawrie. Sculpture panels act as an intermediary between the monumental exterior of the building and its richly decorated interior spaces.

Opposite Rockefeller Center, New York, by Raymond Hood and others, 1931. As uncompromising as a piece of abstract sculpture, the building is stripped of all historical reference or surface decoration; it relies for its impact on the play of light across its surface and the sheer scale of its silhouette against the sky.

Right Empire State Building, New York, by Shreve, Lamb & Harmon, 1932. Despite its air of optimism, this building was out of date by the time it was built as its sheer height in relation to its width rendered it impractical. However, it still expressed the aspirations of its time in a way that a more functional building could not.

Above and right **Chrysler Building, New York, by William Van Alen, 1928–30.** In contrast to the Rockefeller Center, this building is a richly decorated structure, culminating in a pinnacled crown. Its glittering surface and sculptural ornament are references to Chrysler cars.

Above Nebraska State
Capitol, Lincoln, designed by
Bertram Goodhue, 1922–32.
The simplified classical
quality of this building made
it the prototype for much of
the public architecture of the
period, constructed under the
aegis of the Public Works
Administration during the
Depression.

Right Lobby, Chrysler Building, by William Van Alen, 1928. The exterior decoration of this building relates to that of an automobile and the foyer has similar associations, for cars of the period inevitably had wood veneer on the dashboard and wood trim on the doors.

Left Elevator door, Chrysler Building. The Egyptian elements of the exterior are restated here in the stylized lotus flower, and the whole design is related to the exterior pinnacle.

Above Radiator grille, Chanin Building, New York, by Jacques Delamarre, 1927. As with all skyscrapers, aspects of modern technology— electric lights and radiator grilles—had to be incorporated into the decorative scheme. Here the stepped motif represents the ziggurat-shaped exterior, and the wavy lines suggest energy.

Right Executive suite, Chanin Building, New York, by Jacques Delamarre, 1929. Domestic bathrooms of this period tended to be utilitarian, but here the heating and electric lighting are luxurious; the opulent decoration is based on Egyptian motifs.

Right 'Nicotine' wallpaper for the Men's Smoking Room, Radio City Music Hall. The formalization of the motifs in this design owes an obvious debt to Raoul Dufy, but the humour implicit in the colour (nicotine yellow and brown) and the choice of objects, symbolizing men without women, is very American.

Left Ladies Powder Room, Radio City Music Hall, by Yasuo Kuniyoshi. The interiors of the Rockefeller Center are the work of several designers. In this deliberately fantastic creation, the furniture and mirrors appear to float against the painted walls, an impression emphasized by the lack of a defined boundary between the wall and ceiling.

Above **Restroom, Rockefeller Center, by Eugene Schoen. Though employing glass and metal furniture similar to that used by Yasuo Kuniyoshi, Schoen creates a very different effect, one of modernity and opulence, with the Cubist-inspired wallpaper and upholstered chairs.**

Left **'Skyscraper' bookcase designed by Paul Frankl, 1925–30. Frankl believed that furniture should reflect the specifically American identity of skyscrapers. His multi-functional designs were highly influential in the following decade.**

Below Private suite for S.L. Rothafel, Radio City Music Hall, by Donald Deskey, 1930s. The chromed lamps, with their emphatic joints, and the metal frames of the desk and chairs are a sophisticated adaptation of the Bauhaus machine aesthetic. The overall effect is modern but opulent.

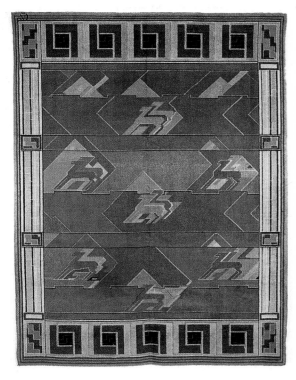

Above Carpets designed by
Maja Andersson Wirde and
woven in the studio of Loja
Saarinen, 1932. The
monochrome colouring is
derived from Cubist painting,
but the designs are Pre-
Columbian in inspiration —
the stylized animals from
textiles and the pyramid from
architecture.

Above Barnsdall (Hollyhock) house, Los Angeles, by Frank Lloyd Wright, 1917. From the beginning of his career Wright had been interested in Pre-Columbian art and architecture. This house, constructed of concrete, is one of his first experiments with Maya forms.

Right **Trylon and Perisphere, New York World's Fair, by Wallace Harrison and J. André Fouilhoux, 1939. Bridging the disciplines of architecture and sculpture, this was the central motif of the Fair. Visitors rode in what was then the world's longest escalator part-way up the Trylon (symbolic of limitless flight) and then crossed by ramp to the Perisphere (symbolic of controlled stasis). Streamlining played an important role in the architecture of the Fair and in its futuristic installations.**

Left Ford Pavilion, New York World's Fair, by Walter Dorwin Teague, 1939. Seen from above, this building with its spiralling test ramp assumed the shape of a gear lever. Nearby, Bel Geddes's General Motors building contained a diorama of the city of the future, in the year 1960.

Right and opposite In streamlined buildings the flexibility of the pre-fabricated metal components gave rise to some extraordinary structures, derived more from science fiction than traditional architecture. It also made possible some notable examples of integrated decoration. In the building opposite the free-form race track is both a decorative element *and* the door and window frames.

Above Guggenheim Museum, New York, designed by Frank Lloyd Wright in 1942 and built fifteen years later. The sweeping streamlined form of the Guggenheim Museum seems closer to some futuristic machine than traditional architecture.

Right Desk and chair designed by Frank Lloyd Wright for the Johnson Wax Building, 1936–9. The forms of this furniture echo the shape of the building, and the use of metal reflects Wright's commitment to technology.

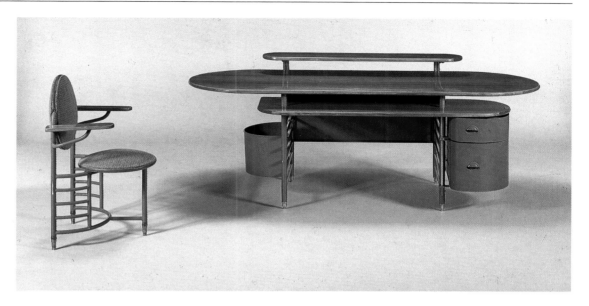

Left Johnson Wax Building, Racine, Wisconsin, by Frank Lloyd Wright, 1936–9. In this, the first of Wright's curvilinear buildings, the walls surge towards the entrance. This impression of a vortex is heightened by the stacked concentric disks of the tower.

Left Cooler and tray designed by Henry Dreyfuss around 1936. The smooth shape and swept-back handle demonstrate the application of streamlining to a domestic object.

Right: City of Salina, M10000, 1936. Re-styled in accordance with Bel Geddes's designs for streamlined trains, this diesel-powered, lightweight locomotive was also technologically advanced. The bodywork was rich brown with a vivid band of yellow sweeping back from the cab.

Left Cord '812 Phaeton' designed by Gordon M. Buchrig and built by Auburn Automobile Co., 1937. The Cord 'Phaeton' is a perfect example of cosmetic streamlining. While not in any sense truly aerodynamic, it suggests power and speed.

Below Scale designed for Toledo Scale by Norman Bel Geddes, 1929. Bel Geddes's concept of streamlining as 'a single unit of uninterrupted flowing line' could be applied to cars, furniture and product design.

Right Radio of wood, metal and blue glass, by Walter Dorwin Teague, 1936. In contrast to the phonograph on page 158 this is an emphatically modern design, but the streamlining merely symbolizes the technological function of the radio, rather than relating to the physical demands of the radio housing.

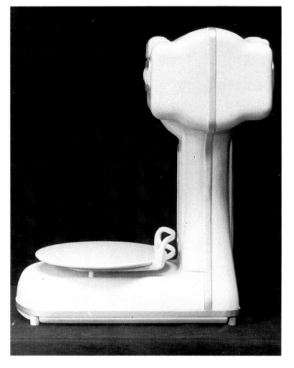

Below Entrance hall of Syrie Maugham's own house in London, about 1939. This theatrical use of antique furniture and decoration found its way into set design. The overpainting of the furniture is a deliberate negation of historical authenticity.

Above Bathroom designed for a De Mille film of the early 1930s. This, with its classical pilasters and restrained ornament, is a free adaptation of Robsjohn-Gibbings' work.

Above A scene from *The Golddiggers of 1933*, by Busby Berkeley, 1935. Berkeley's highly organized choreography creates geometric patterns which are clearly related to the formalizations of Deco.

Left: *Cleopatra*, with costumes by Travis Banton, Cecil B. De Mille for Paramount, 1934. In this glamorous fantasy of ancient Egypt the whole effect recalls the Chrysler Building: the sphinx is paralleled by the hubcap sculpture and the glitter, the patterns and the head-dresses evoke the same spirit as the tower.

Left Greta Garbo in an Adrian
costume for *Mata Hari*,
M.G.M., 1932, and (*above*)
The Girls, gilt-bronze and
ivory figures by Demetre
Chiparus. In sheathing his
Mata Hari in metal so only
her face and hands emerge,
Adrian is clearly inspired by
Chiparus's slightly perverse
figures.

5/MASS PRODUCTION

Although the style promoted by the Arts and Crafts movement did find its way into mass-produced goods, the general ethos of the movement did little to enhance the image of mass production. At the beginning of the century the term, when applied to furniture and decorative objects, tended to evoke images of shoddy, badly designed items made for those who could not afford the 'real thing'. In advertising from the first two decades of the twentieth century the words 'unique', 'crafted' and 'traditional' are used, particularly by manufacturers of middle- to lower-price-range products who obviously felt the need to play down the part of the machine in their production.

Traditional designs, which formed the largest part in the repertoire of most furniture companies in America and Europe, were not on the whole improved by being mass-produced; the distinguishing features of 'Colonial', 'Tudor' or 'Georgian' furniture were debased, and cheap materials were masked by an over-application of decoration. It was not until the twenties that materials which were man-made, or rather machine-made, began to gain any credibility in the applied arts, and forms which owed their origins to mass production rather than tradition then began to present a real alternative to the crafted, precious item.

As a style, Art Deco was uniquely well suited to mass production. At least part of its design language, even in the earliest and most luxurious phase, was derived from the machine aesthetic, though at this stage references to machine form were merely part of the great avalanche of stylistic influences which were fed into Deco in the early twenties. In the later twenties and thirties, the machine element of Deco design became increasingly important as mass production became a necessity and designers recognized the significance of the mass market.

This recognition brought about quite radical changes in marketing and a corresponding boom in advertising, particularly in America. In 1915 magazines and periodicals carried only twenty-five million dollars' worth of advertising; by 1929 it was up to one hundred and fifty million dollars. The nature of the advertisements changed too. At the beginning of the century advertising copy simply described what was available, but by the end of the twenties it was working on a much more complex level, extolling the virtues of one product over all comparable products and persuading people to buy what they could do without. The twenties and thirties saw the rise of several large advertising agencies, including J. Walter Thompson and Calkins & Holden.

The increasing sophistication of the market requiring mass-produced items forced manufacturers to consult with their retail outlets over the precise nature of their consumers' demands. The middle classes, which composed such a vital part of the buying public, wanted well designed or, at least, fashionable objects. But while American manufacturers were well in advance of their European counterparts in their readiness to respond to market needs, and while many of them had the equipment and technology to supply such a demand, they rarely had any idea of how to utilize up-to-date design ideas. In 1929 no less than five hundred manufacturers applied to the New York Art Center for artists and designers to update their products.

By the later twenties the term 'mass production' had ceased to imply simply the large-scale manufacturing by machines of objects which had hitherto been made by hand: it now described objects which had no previous history, new consumer items like radios, refrigerators, cameras and so on which owed their existence entirely to machine processes and were made in quantity from the beginning. The term could also be extended to include architecture. Though mass-produced architecture, in the sense of identical buildings being repeated endlessly, was hardly new, the idea of a deliberate multiple in a style unique to a particular company was. Both commerce and the entertainment industry saw the possibilities inherent in this 'house style', in which a building belonging to a particular company, no matter where it was located, could be identified at once as being 'Burton's the Tailors', an Odeon cinema, or, in America, a Texaco gas station. The same idea was extended to public services, and the London Public Transport Board for instance, under Frank Pick, created a distinctive house style in their stations by Charles Holden, their graphics by Edward Johnston and their furnishings.

Another new area of design, one which expanded rapidly throughout the twenties and thirties, was the automobile. When Henry Ford produced his 'Model T' he intended it to be the ultimate car, so cheap and so simple that almost anyone could afford and operate one. The appearance of the 'Model T' was of secondary importance to Ford, who had no serious rival in the popular car market until 1923 when Chevrolet produced a model which was both cheap and stylish. Mechanically this was very similar to the 'Model T', but visually it had more in common with the kind of styling which had hitherto only been found on much more expensive and exclusive cars like the Pierce 'Arrow'. As early as 1916 William B. Stout, then body engineer for Scripps-Booth, had said, 'Art is the science of eye appeal', predicting that the car of the future would 'use art lines to suggest the action of the mechanism'. Chevrolet responded to this with their 1923 model, at a time when the market was saturated by Ford's 'Model T'. The Chevrolet was a great success, not because it worked better but because it looked better; women particularly liked it because it was infinitely more glamorous than the stubby, basic Ford.

General Motors responded to the success of the Chevrolet by introducing a wide range of colours for their cars, based on Du Pont's newly developed synthetic resins, and by hiring in 1926 Harley J. Earl, a car customizer, to work as a designer in their Cadillac division. His 1929 'La Salle' was such a success, with its stylish unified design, rounded corners and low silhouette, that Earl was put in charge of a team of designers and made responsible for the styling of General Motors' whole range. Under pressure, Ford produced the 'Model A Phaeton' which was launched in 1927 with seven body styles and eight colours. It was an object lesson to the automobile industry, not because it was innovative in any way, but because Ford had really changed so little and the success of the car was due to its advertising.

Chrysler were experimenting with wind tunnel tests on prototype designs in 1927 and by the thirties both they and General Motors were toying with the idea of a streamlined car based on the ideas in Bel Geddes's book *Horizons*. Chrysler produced the streamlined 'Airflow' in 1934. Designed by Frank M. Zelder, it featured integrated fenders, headlights incorporated into the body and a continual curving line between the nose and the hood. Bel Geddes in his publicity for the model described it as the 'first real motor car'. What he actually meant was that it *looked* like the first real motor car because it was deliberately styled to evoke images of speed and aerodynamics, unlike most of its contemporaries whose design was still derived from that of horse-drawn carriages. In fact, the original design had to be modified because the technology of Chrysler's engines was less advanced than the design of the body.

Throughout the twenties and early thirties the actual mechanics of cars changed very little, but their appearance did, and the evolution of car design on both sides of the Atlantic became the evolution of body style, the way a car looked rather than the way it performed. Ford had designed the 'Model T' to last for ever, but now, in a rapidly growing consumer society, the public had other priorities. Shrewd advertising by such firms as Calkins & Holden had no trouble in persuading customers to change their cars regularly rather than drive them until they fell apart.

The technology of the automobile industry influenced other areas of design. The use of colour, for instance, and improvements in finishes for metals were both applied to the furniture industry. Metals of various sorts had been used in the construction of furniture for centuries, both as an extremely versatile decorative element and as a structural component. In the early twenties, Deco designers such as Christofle, Edgar Brandt and Armand Rateau continued to use metals in the traditional way and metal furniture and objects were, in fact, some of the most decorative items in the 1925 Paris Exhibition. The first pieces of metal furniture to employ the material in a new way and explore its potential in mass production were German, but since Germany did not exhibit at the Exhibition the direct influence of Breuer and van der Rohe was probably felt most strongly in America, where designers like Donald Deskey and Joseph Urban produced slightly more modish and luxurious versions of the Bauhaus originals. In France the first pieces of tubular steel furniture to be made for a mass market were manufactured by DIM (Décoration Intérieur Moderne), a firm founded in 1919 by René Joubert. Critical reaction to furniture of this type was not enthusiastic, the most frequently expressed fear being that the use of tubular steel would destroy any individual character in furniture design and render everything as clinical as hospital equipment.

By 1928 the firm of Thonet, which had been making mass-produced bentwood furniture since the 1850s, began producing tubular steel pieces to designs by Le Corbusier. In 1930 they opened their first showroom in England, to be followed the year after by PEL (Practical Equipment Ltd.), a branch of Tube Investments. Of these companies only early DIM retained much of the austerity of Bauhaus design; both Thonet and PEL turned the machined, slightly clinical quality of the chromed metal to positive advantage by contrasting it with rich upholstery, leathers and suedes, and with interesting surfaces of black glass, bakelite or even marble. The result is very modern and very luxurious. Just as Deskey's pieces in the States were bought by a fairly wealthy clientele, DIM, PEL and Thonet were able to appeal to a cultured and monied buying public.

The basic forms of this luxurious tubular furniture were adapted during the thirties to true mass production without compromise of the sort which had traditionally rendered mass-produced furniture second-rate. The luxurious upholstery tended to be replaced by canvas, but this did not alter the basic line of the furniture or its quality. Literally any sort of furniture could be made from tubular metal; in the thirties PEL was producing hospital, hotel and catering furniture and equipment, as well as the ubiquitous stacking chairs which must surely qualify as the most universal manifestation of any style since the beginning of time.

In the States mass-produced metal furniture followed the same transition from stylish luxury to equally stylish restraint. Design for mass production came from two separate sources: from Deco designers who had already been using the material, and from the relatively new area of industrial design, but there is little visual difference between the products of the two disciplines. Kem Weber's furniture from 1934 for the Lloyd manufacturing company and Raymond Loewy's designs for office furniture share an identical language, although Weber was a designer in the traditional and accepted sense while Loewy was basically an industrial designer, responsible for, among other things, the Greyhound buses of the thirties.

Before turning the bulk of its production to metal furniture, Thonet had specialized in plywood pieces—it was one of the first companies to explore the potential of this material in mass production. Laminated woods had been developed in Finland in 1890 and the process was subsequently made more efficient and cheaper in the States, so by the beginning of this century three-ply plywood was in general use. Although available in a number of finishes, it was not used for furniture and was considered more suitable for doors and other flat surfaces. In fact, it was infinitely flexible and had one great advantage over metal: it was both machine-made and traditional, with all the 'friendly' qualities associated with wood.

As might be expected, there was plenty of badly made and visually offensive plywood furniture, and many manufacturers used it as a cheap substitute for solid wood instead of exploiting its own special properties. The designer Alvar Aalto, on the other hand, made a range of pieces which featured the smooth, curving lines and particular strengths of the material. It could, like metal, be cantilevered; and in his work the machined quality of ply is used to emphasize the sculptural element of the design. His work was enormously influential in Europe and America in the thirties, when metal was used in the manner of ply in truly mass-produced furniture and in limited-production luxury pieces, which were still machine-made but for a much smaller market.

In almost every area of mass-produced design America was in advance of both England and the Continent. Design was encouraged on several levels: the Metropolitan Museum, for example, used its yearly 'Contemporary Trends' exhibition to show the best of mass-produced furniture, beginning in 1930 when the exhibition featured a proportion of mass-market pieces along with luxury items, and culminating in the show of 1934 which concentrated entirely on pieces which were readily available and reasonably priced. The 1934 exhibition proved to be extremely popular, attracting 39,000 people and giving lie to the idea that no one would want to see a show of such items. On a more practical level, many of the large manufacturing concerns in the States were willing to pay handsomely for good, or at least well known, designers. Norman Bel Geddes could command a thousand dollars to design an item, and Walter Dorwin Teague and Raymond Loewy both worked on retainers of twelve thousand.

On both sides of the Atlantic the fashion for living in flats or apartments was widespread by the twenties and thirties, due in part to the rise of a new professional class who needed to live in the city but were unwilling, or unable, to afford a city house. That this was going to be a permanent fact of modern life was recognized in the States by Russel Wright, who in 1935 extended his 'Modern Living' range of low-priced, mass-produced furniture to include co-ordinated textiles, lamps and rugs. The furniture was constructed from maple, cut very simply into smooth rectangular shapes which were subsequently echoed in the textiles and accessories. Many of the pieces were multi-functional, making them ideal for smaller rooms. 'Modern Living' was sold through Macy's and became a bestseller immediately, so whereas the co-ordinated interior had previously been accessible only to the rich, it was now available to a much wider market.

In Europe most countries were still suffering from the after-effects of the First World War, as well as the Depression. Only in Scandinavia, particularly Sweden which had been neutral in the war and whose industry had never been turned to the war effort, was there an established tradition of co-operation between the designer and industry. The Swedish exhibition of 1930 showed a range of objects, including pieces by Aalto, designed specifically for mass production; these excited favourable comment, especially in England.

In comparison with their American counterparts, English designers earned almost nothing and were seen in industry as a luxury rather than a necessity. In the thirties John Gloag described the products of British industry as being 'fantastically inept', an opinion shared by many others. In an attempt to bring some quality to the mass market, the Royal Academy sponsored a show in 1935 called 'British Art in

Industry'. This was partially inspired by the Swedish exhibition and aimed to 'encourage British artists to give industry the benefits of their talent and training so that the objects with which we are surrounded in our daily lives may have an appearance which is not only attractive but which is based on genuinely artistic principles'. In fact, the exhibition showed very little which had anything to do with mass production; most of the exhibits were costly, with designers like Betty Joel showing work which was certainly exciting and certainly Deco but utterly unsuited to the realities of most people's 'daily lives'.

It is fair to say that in Britain there was no real equivalent to Wright; a true picture of what was available to the general public was to be found not in the Academy but in the Ideal Home exhibition, sponsored each year by the *Daily Mail.* Since there was no selection committee, any and every manufacturer could take a stand and the exhibition epitomized popular interior design. It formed most people's only direct experience of Deco furniture and in the catalogues could be seen the ubiquitous 'three-piece suite' produced by the majority of furniture companies in the thirties. The two chairs and one settee that comprised the suite were usually huge. Their bulky forms incorporated favourite Deco elements—stylized fan shapes, perhaps, or ziggurat feet—and they were often upholstered with Deco fabrics, but not necessarily ones which complemented the overall contours of the furniture.

The later twenties saw the introduction of a new element in the domestic interior: the electric light with its attendant fixtures and fittings. In England particularly, the electric light was not greeted with total enthusiasm for it was expensive and not completely reliable. Design for electricity tended to be either cautiously traditional, in the shape of mock candles, candelabra and chandeliers, or else very utilitarian since a plain glass globe gave the most (and therefore cheapest) light. The American attitude to electricity was rather more forward-looking. Frank Lloyd Wright was one of the first designers to incorporate mechanical services and electric lighting into the domestic interior, and it is significant that Russel Wright should have included a selection of lamps in his 'Modern Living' range.

The best designs in Europe came first from relatively expensive sources. The firm of Lalique was manufacturing a range of lights which were exported in quantity to England, but although they were mass-produced they were still in a price range which made them inaccessible to many people. The influence of Lalique, however, in the area of mass-produced glass cannot be overestimated. The designer had turned his attention from jewellery to glass at the beginning of the century and was already interested in designing for mass production when Coty invited him to produce a range of perfume bottles in 1908. By 1925 the firm of Lalique was mass-producing decorative items of all kinds. Lalique evolved methods of shaping and decorating glass which were particularly suited to the processes of mass production. Etching, which was used on sheet glass for lamps and tables, and moulding, particularly of opalescent glass, were both industrial techniques which

Glass table-lamp with peacock stopper by René Lalique, 1920s.

Light-fitting of sand-blasted glass and satin-finished metal, designed by A.B. Read for Troughton & Young, 1930–32.

Lalique exploited to produce designs of great drama and style. The great strength of his work lay in the fact that he designed specifically for such techniques, so the products of the company are not machine-made copies of hand-engraved or carved originals—the machine-made pieces *are* the originals. The output of the Lalique company was never cheap, but nevertheless it was immensely popular in France, and subsequently in England and America, and both the designs and the techniques were widely imitated. By the mid-thirties, however, much cheaper glass fittings were being imported from Italy and Czechoslovakia, and the home industries began to manufacture more inventive and stylish lamp standards, table-lamps and wall-fittings, often in chrome and glass, or in the highly popular chrome and parchment.

Glass became increasingly important in mass-produced furniture and objects throughout the thirties. The smaller scale of domestic interiors built during the decade made mirrors a useful decorative feature; they threw back light (including expensive electric light) and created an illusion of space. Mirrors had already been used in up-market interior design by people like Deskey, Urban and Frankl—Urban particularly made a motif of the large circular mirror in many of his private design commissions in the thirties—but new technical advances in the manufacturing of glass enabled the cheap production of coloured and opaque glasses, as well as mirrored glass in a variety of pastel shades. British Vitrolite marketed an opaque glass, available in black and made with a ridged back for fixing to other surfaces. The same company marketed 'Vitroflex', an adhesive webbing specifically designed to fix small mirrored tiles to curved surfaces or small objects. By the middle of the thirties mirrors were being used in bathrooms (sometimes to cover a whole wall), on furniture, and on items like cigarette-boxes which had the dual advantage of being glamorous and fairly cheap. The mixture of glass and chrome, particularly when used with one of the new textured wall paints, became the standard decorative language of cafés and less elaborate picture houses by the end of the decade.

Glass was cheaper to mass-produce than ceramics, and during the Depression glassware became perhaps the most readily available aspect of Deco design. In America some established manufacturers, Steuben for example, elected to turn their backs on the mass market and concentrate on exclusive pieces sold through limited outlets. Others, like Indiana Glass, the Hazel Atlas Glass Company and Hocking Glass, turned their manufacturing processes completely to the production of what became known as 'Depression' glass. Most items sold for a few cents or were given away as premiums with another product, much as mugs and glasses are now given away with petrol. Some furniture stores would offer a whole dinner- or tea-service as a premium when a customer bought a suite of dining-room furniture, and some movie-house chains had 'glassware nights' when the price of an entrance ticket included a piece of Depression glass. Indiana Glass, Hazel Atlas and Hocking all manufactured glassware in pastel shades and in shapes derived from the Deco vocabulary. Depression glass was never intended to be anything other than 'cheap and cheerful'. None of the manufacturers attempted to imitate cut glass, but concentrated instead on novelty of design; the 'Tea Room' pattern by Indiana Glass, for example, was octagonal in shape while their 'Pyramid' pattern was based on inverted triangles.

The manufacturers of mass-produced glassware were quick to recognize new trends. When refrigerators became available to the mass market in the mid-thirties, the manufacturers of Depression glass increased their ranges to include 'ice-box furniture'; on the repeal of Prohibition they produced cocktail-shakers and other bar equipment. Glassware of this type, which was available on both sides of the Atlantic, is treated with very little respect by design historians, if it is mentioned at all. But it was this kind of mass production, and this type of object, which ensured the longevity of the Deco style. In the end it is not the high quality, expensively mass-produced items which the Lalique factory was exporting, nor even the items which Lalique designed for Coty, which are popularly seen as 'Deco'. These objects still only reached a very limited section of the population, while Depression glass, on the other hand, reached everyone without becoming a cheap imitation of an exclusive 'original'.

Liqueur decanter and glasses, 1920s.

Ceramics like glassware reached a wide public in the twenties and thirties. Some of it is only 'Deco' because Deco patterns were transfer-printed onto traditional shapes, the end result being an unhappy marriage between geometric 'jazz' patterns and curving silhouettes. A number of established firms in America and Europe, however, gave serious attention to the problem of mass-producing a good-quality product in the new style, and to this end Wedgwood employed an architect, Keith Murray, to design for them in the thirties. The ranges produced by Murray were simple in shape, co-ordinated by the decorative use of horizontal banding and by the colours, which were all muted tints and hues rather than primaries. The quality of the pieces made to Murray's designs had to be high because the absolute simplicity of the shapes, and the lack of any applied decoration, made any kind of disguise impossible. Nevertheless, the pieces sold for very reasonable prices, the cheapest item in the range, an ash-tray, retailing for as little as one shilling and six pence, and they were popular, having the virtue of being modern without being aggressively so.

Indiana glass from a 1930s catalogue. This highly popular 'Depression' glass, though hardly subtle, was brightly coloured, inventive and cheap.

The same might be said of the work produced by Susie Cooper from the Crown Works, Burslem. Her mass-produced dinner, tea and coffee sets were again of very high quality and she led a team of decorators who were so consistent in their work that damaged pieces from a set could be matched and replaced some years after that set had first appeared on the market. In her designs for mass production Susie Cooper concentrated on useful, adaptable shapes which, like Murray's, were modern but restrained. Because of this her work adapted itself from decade to decade with very little change in basic outline.

Arthur J. Wilkinson was the firm for which Clarice Cliff worked in the thirties, designing her 'Bizarre' ware along with more conservative designs like 'Crocus'. Unlike Susie Cooper's the power of her work lies in the decoration rather than the actual shape of her pieces. 'Bizarre' derives from a number of sources—primitive art, Futurism, Cubism and Russian folk art—and it was painted by a team of decorators in sufficient quantities for it to be retailed through large department stores, Lawley's and even Woolworth's in the thirties. Other potteries concentrated on the production of decorative objects rather than services and sets. James Sadler & Sons made a range of angled vases and bookends, Newport Potteries, who employed Clarice Cliff after 1939, made vases, plaques and candlesticks, while Beswick produced decorative wall masks, enormously popular in the thirties. Shelley, who made china rather than pottery, produced the highly successful 'Vogue' pattern, stylish in silhouette and decoration.

In retrospect the British potteries coped better with mass production than contemporary critics would have us believe. The work of Murray, Cooper and Cliff was sufficiently admired on the Continent to be imitated, and many potteries were turning out designs which were inventive and witty. Yet no designer either in Britain or on the Continent approached the phenomenal success of Russel Wright, who devised the 'American Modern' ceramic range in 1937. He based the individual pieces on a mixture of traditional and streamlined forms and produced the range in a number of colours which were supposed to be 'mixed and matched'. After some initial problems Wright persuaded the Steubenville potteries to manufacture the design, which became probably the best selling line of ceramics ever. It was re-designed slightly in 1949 for the international market and thereafter sold well in Europe throughout the fifties. The initial success of this range was so great that the stores which sold it were quite unable to keep pace with demand, and the Steubenville potteries doubled their size entirely on the strength of 'American Modern'.

The Homer Laughlin company produced two best-selling lines, 'Harlequin' and 'Fiesta', both of which were retailed from the mid-thirties to the sixties. 'Harlequin' was intended for retail through Woolworth's and was cheaper than 'Fiesta', although neither was expensive. Both ranges have important design elements in common with Murray's work for Wedgwood in England: the use of moulded concentric circles on the plates and horizontal bands on serving dishes, beakers, and vases to emphasize the shape; also the machined quality of the pieces. Both 'Harlequin' and 'Fiesta', however, were brightly coloured and like 'American Modern' were made to mix and match. Many cheap lines of pottery in the States, including 'Harlequin', were, like Depression glass, given away as premiums, particularly with kitchen appliances.

Plastics never posed a serious threat to the ceramics industry in the Deco period. Plastic tableware made in America and England had the advantage of being impervious to boiling water and almost unbreakable in normal use, but unfortunately the type of plastic most suitable for tableware was limited in its colour. It came in a range of rather unappetizing mottled shades which did little to enhance the food served on it, so during the thirties its use was restricted to picnic ware.

The great strength of plastic as a material lay in its absolute adaptability. The range of completely synthetic materials increased in the thirties and manufacturers like Imperial Chemical Industries developed techniques for making sheet plastic which could be heat-moulded into almost any shape. Lucite, Catalin and Plexiglass were used for a number of items from jewellery through cigarette-boxes and vanity sets to radios and furniture. The novelty aspect of these materials was utilized by designers like Elsie de Wolfe and Cora Scovill, both of whom designed furniture in the transparent Plexiglass, but their true value lay in their complete suitability for mass production. The 'Fada Baby' radio in America was housed in a plastic case and able to change its design and colours year by year; in England, bakelite was used for radio bodies from the late twenties, perhaps the best example being Wells Coates' 'AD65' model from the mid-thirties with its circular case. There are innumerable examples of the inventive use of plastics from the Deco period, but many of the designers are anonymous. We do not know who designed the cream cigarette-boxes with lids moulded in imitation of low-relief sculpture, which were so popular on both sides of the Atlantic in the thirties, nor who designed the bulk of the plastic jewellery, cocktail equipment and early plastic packaging. In the end it hardly matters. The material was new enough to be chic simply because of its novelty, and cheap enough to be available to every one. It was the perfect material for the expression of streamlined Deco, and plastic items carried the style well into the post-war period.

The idea of something which was cheap also being fashionable first appears in the Deco period. Previously, fashion had been the prerogative of the wealthy, who were happy to pay for expensive materials and exclusive designs, and by the time a particular style had filtered down through the various social levels the innovators were moving on to new ideas, new lines and new materials. One designer, Chanel, particularly captures the modern spirit in fashion during the twenties and thirties. 'Coco' Chanel popularized the notion of plastic jewellery and was also responsible for producing a range of clothes which were so simple in their basic lines and fabrics that it was possible for almost anyone who had a sewing machine to copy them at home, and for retail chains to produce inexpensive reproductions. Unlike most couturiers, Chanel was happy to see her clothes being copied for, as she said, fashion does not exist unless it goes down into the streets'. Her own 'ready to wear' clothes were obviously too expensive for the average woman but her basic ideas of using sports clothes, including trousers, for day wear and adapting items of masculine clothing, adding white collars and cuffs to the cardigan for instance, could be copied by anyone. Her influence can be seen by looking through any woman's magazine from the period, not just *Vogue* or *Harper's* but also the cheaper weekly papers aimed at a middle- or working-class readership. The hints for home dressmakers in such magazines are full of references to Chanel.

The increase in advertising and the growth of the popular media in the shape of papers, magazines, the radio and the movies had a profound influence on fashion. The sewing machine, too, had a democratizing effect, begun some twenty years before, and the growth of the paper-pattern industry in the twenties took this process further. A woman could make for herself the kind of clothes she saw in the papers or on the screen, and by the thirties the time-lapse between an item's first appearance in a film or photograph and its becoming common property was very short. Clothes were, of course, mass-produced as the garment industry turned out fashion in quantity on every level from cheaply made items to the more expensive hand-finished clothes which retailed to the new middle-class professional market. In another sense, however, it was fashion ideas that were being mass-produced and belonged to everyone, not simply to those who were wealthy enough to afford fashion-houses or the services of a professional couturier.

In both fashion and domestic goods there was an enormous output of mass-produced Deco which falls into the category outlined at the beginning of this chapter, cheap imitations of expensive orginals. Small domestic items and personal accessories used nickel plating for silver and transfer printing for enamel; plastic was made to look like ivory, coral or jade. Much of this can be described as 'make-believe glamour', the glamour of the movies. It is easy to dismiss this area of mass production as rubbish but it fulfilled a need, just as the lavish musical spectaculars did on celluloid, to escape from reality, particularly in the Depression. Furthermore, mass production brought fashion to those of modest means for the first time, so playing an important part in the democratization of culture that has characterized this century.

Right Jubilee cinema, Swanscombe, 1930s. In even the most impoverished areas the simple local cinemas were enlivened by typically Deco decoration.

Left and below Odeon cinemas, 1930s, interior, Muswell Hill, and exterior, Weston-super-Mare. Like the Texaco gas stations, the Odeon cinemas shared a readily identifiable house style, though they were not identical in design. More than any other building type, cinemas came to be associated in the public mind with the Art Deco style.

Above Texaco gas station, Type C, Walter Dorwin Teague, 1930s. By the forties Texaco had five hundred Type C gas stations across America. Each had the same green, white and red colour scheme and an identical rectangular plan, with a projecting canopy to shelter the pumps and carry the sign.

Left Osterley station designed by Charles Holden, 1935. Frank Pick, the commercial manager of London Underground Railways, commissioned Holden to design the stations for the underground system. Although there is no 'house style' in the Texaco sense, there is a strong group identity in these stations.

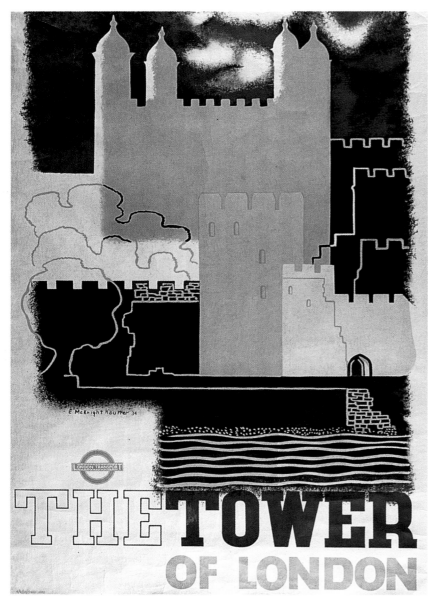

Above and right Posters for London Transport by E. McKnight Kauffer, 1934. Frank Pick also commissioned a range of artists to design posters for London Underground Railways. Most of the artists were to break away from traditional illustration to experiment with forms derived from modern painting.

Below Poster for London Transport by K. Burrell.

Above Hupmobile Sedan designed by Raymond Loewy, 1934. As a practical demonstration of his ideas Loewy built a streamlined body onto a Hupmobile chassis at his own expense.

Left Chrysler 'Airflow' designed by Frank M. Zelder, 1936. This was the first car seriously to embody streamlining but, despite all efforts to make it truly aerodynamic, the ideal teardrop shape was rendered impossible by the heavy engines which had to be placed at the front.

Above Ford 'Model A', 1928, and (*right*) 'Model F Tourer', 1932. Ford's 'Model T' had dominated the American market until 1923, but car buyers were now demanding style as well as function and the 'Model T' began to look old fashioned. The 'Model A', though innovative in appearance only, was a great success.

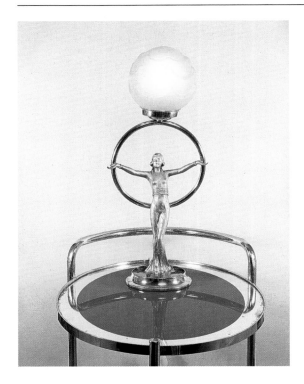

Above Table lamp, chrome and glass, with gilded spelter lady; tubular steel table, 1920s. Lighting was an integral part of Deco interior design and by the late twenties table and standard lamps were available on the mass market. The Chiparus-inspired lady is a typical example of the adaptation of exclusive items to the mass market.

Right The self-consciously chic décor is a popular interpretation of the ideas of designers like Denham MacLaren and Syrie Maugham. It contains all the essentials of the modern interior—the cocktail-cabinet, the aggressively modernist fireplace, the chrome standard lamp and the zebra-pattern rug.

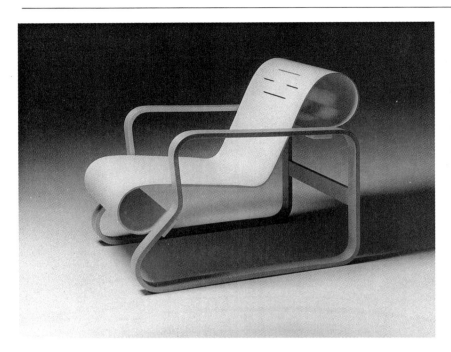

Left Chair of laminated birch and veneered plywood, designed by Alvar Aalto, 1932. This chair, for the Paimio Sanatorium of which Aalto was the architect, is an experiment in tonal contrasts, with natural wood set against painted surfaces. It is still in production, manufactured by Artek.

Right The manufacturers of mass-produced furniture were quick to adapt features of modernism, sometimes with bizarre results.

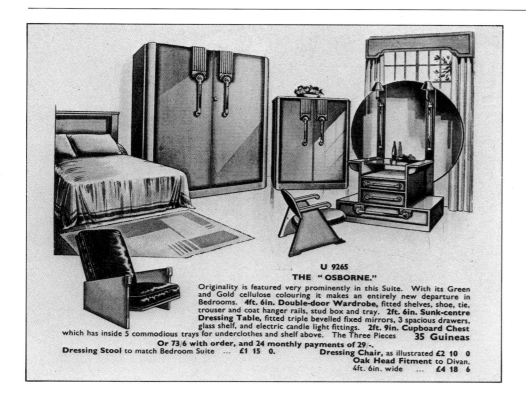

U 9265

THE " OSBORNE."

Originality is featured very prominently in this Suite. With its Green and Gold cellulose colouring it makes an entirely new departure in Bedrooms. **4ft. 6in. Double-door Wardrobe**, fitted shelves, shoe, tie, trouser and coat hanger rails, stud box and tray. **2ft. 6in. Sunk-centre Dressing Table**, fitted triple bevelled fixed mirrors, 3 spacious drawers, glass shelf, and electric candle light fittings. **2ft. 9in. Cupboard Chest** which has inside 5 commodious trays for underclothes and shelf above. The Three Pieces **35 Guineas**

Or 73/6 with order, and 24 monthly payments of 29/-.

Dressing Stool to match Bedroom Suite ... **£1 15 0.**   **Dressing Chair**, as illustrated **£2 10 0**

Oak Head Fitment to Divan, 4ft. 6in. wide ... **£4 18 6**

Above Page from a catalogue issued in the early 1930s by Oetzmann & Co. Ltd., London. This bedroom suite is obviously inspired by the precious metal and lacquer furniture associated with French Deco, although here cellulose is used to imitate lacquer.

Right Page from a catalogue by Footman, Bower & Co. Ltd., around 1937. This type of furniture, of traditional materials and with forms derived from French Deco, was popular with the mass market.

Right Dining-room, Ideal Home exhibition, 1931. Truly mass-market furniture could be found in the Daily Mail Ideal Home exhibition. The chrome-and-glass table has stylistic links with both European and American modernism.

Left 'Modern Living' furniture designed by Russel Wright, 1935. The simple shapes and solid maple construction of Wright's furniture ensured its success in America.

Above **1930s room set in the
Geffrye Museum, London. The
room is an accurate
representation of everyday,
domestic Deco in the thirties.
The influence of mainstream
design can still be
recognized but much of the
furniture simply has Deco
motifs grafted onto shapes
which are not Deco.**

Above Bathroom designed by
Paul Nash for Tilly Losch,
1932. Although this is a
unique interior, the elements
of which it is composed are
mass-produced. The lighting,
far from being utilitarian, has
become an important
decorative element, making
patterns to emphasize
the shape of the room.

Right Bathroom at Claridge's Hotel, London, 1930s. In this lavish interior stock ceiling globes have become part of the decorative scheme. They, and the mirror tiles, are tinted to echo the pink tiles and paint, and to flatter the user of the room.

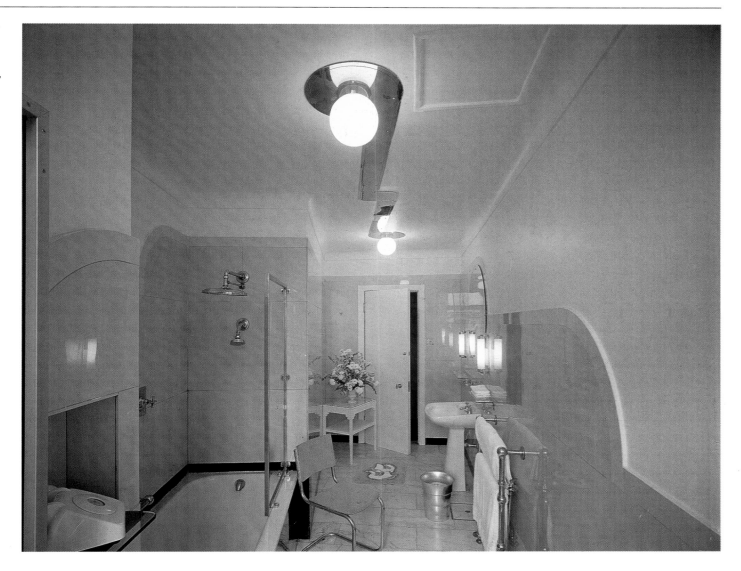

Above Daily Express Building, London, by Sir Owen Williams, 1936–9. The upwardly directed lighting emphasizes the fluting and zigzag moulding, and without it this interior would seem quite flat.

Above Silver Entrance, Park
Lane Hotel, London, 1927. In
Europe and America lighting
was often an integral part of
the decorative scheme,
creating much of the impact
of the design.

Above **Foyer, Strand Palace Hotel, London, 1930s. In this magical combination of reflecting surfaces and diffused light the same stepped shapes are repeated in a variety of shapes, with glass predominating.**

Below Oddeninos' café, London by Yates, Cook & Derbyshire. With its complex series of shapes and illusionary spaces, the interior of Oddeninos' is a perfect example of the use of lighting and reflecting surfaces in Deco interiors.

Above Hoover Building, Perivale, London, by Wallis, Gilbert & Partners, 1932. While the architecture has some affinities with the Modern Movement and the work of Le Corbusier, the decoration belongs to the popular and commercial zigzag Deco style.

RECEPTION OFFICE

Above and left Entrance and detail, Hoover Building. The use of ceramics was common as a decorative element in architecture in Britain in the twenties and thirties, but this is an unusually rich and flamboyant example.

Below Vase designed by Keith Murray for Wedgwood, 1930s. This range, aimed for a mass market and modestly priced, is characterized by simple forms, restrained colours and decorative banding, as befits Murray's training as an architect.

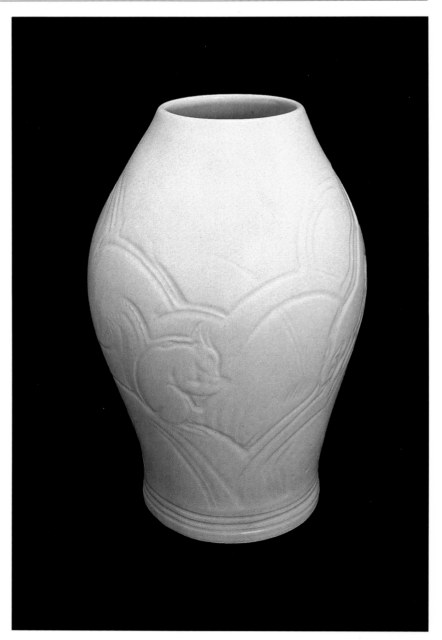

Above 'Squirrel' vase designed by Susie Cooper, 1930s. Despite its handmade appearance, the 'Squirrel' vase was mass produced and available in a number of colours including blue and green. Susie Cooper's work in the thirties was less flamboyant than Clarice Cliff's but she was equally aware of the modern trends in painting.

Below Vegetable dish and plate, part of a dinner service by Susie Cooper for Crown Works, Burslem, 1930s. The shape of this service proved so popular that, with variations in the painted decoration, it was in production until the fifties. The lid of the dish is similarly decorated on the underside and can be reversed for use as a separate dish.

Right Plate and (*above*) 'Lucerne' wall plaque designed by Clarice Cliff, 1930s. Cliff was trained at Burslem Art School before joining A.J. Wilkinson for whom she worked until the end of the thirties. Her work was very popular and the wall plaques particularly enjoyed great favour as wedding presents.

Below 'American Modern' dinnerware designed by Russel Wright for the Steubenville potteries, 1937. This was possibly the most successful line of ceramics ever produced. By the mid-forties Wright was designing a range of glassware, cutlery and tablelinen to accompany the dinner service.

Above and opposite 'Fiesta' and 'Harlequin' ware, manufactured by Homer Laughlin from around 1935 to the 1960s. The most widely available Deco dinnerware, these ceramics came in simple shapes and bright colours, designed to be mixed and matched.

Above and opposite below
**Plastics were used to imitate
more costly natural
materials. Ivory and
tortoiseshell were the two
most frequently copied and
there are innumerable
examples of the fake ivory
and tortoiseshell dressing-
table accessories popular in
the early part of the century.**

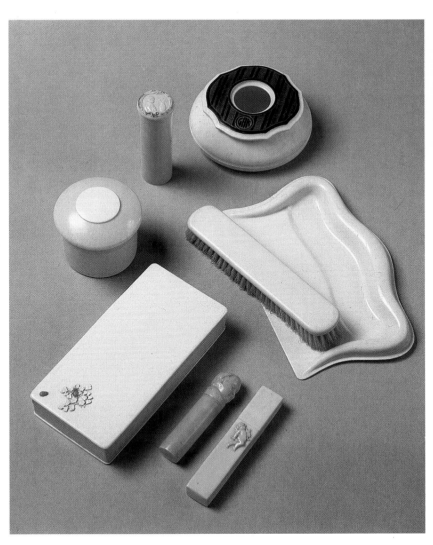

Above Carved plastic boxes, late 1920s. The most expensive method of treating plastic was to hand carve it, so these are strictly speaking luxury items in which plastic is used in the manner traditional to ivory.

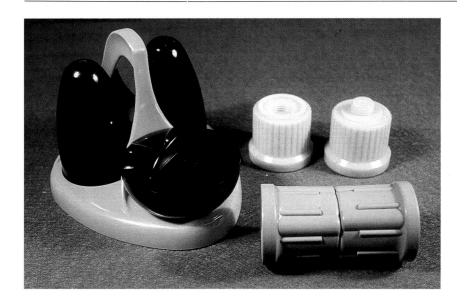

Left Moulded plastic condiment sets. By the early thirties the plastics industry had overcome some of the early problems relating to colour and were able to produce the clear, bright colours that the public desired.

Right Urea milk jugs, tea pots and cups, late 1920s. As urea was machine made and inexpensive, it was hoped that such plastic tableware would rival ceramics. The limited colour range, however, proved a serious disadvantage.

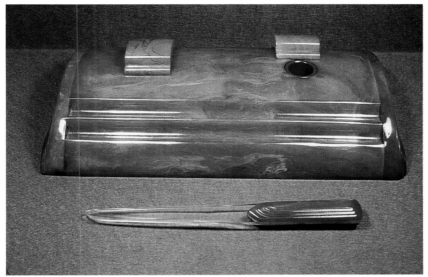

Above Cast phenolic pen-
and-ink tray, 1940s. In
America plastics tended to
be cast, since the process
was cheap and versatile.
This pen-and-ink tray is
formed of one piece with no
seams or joins.

Bandalasta

Left Bandalasta catalogue,
1928. The Bandalasta range
was extensive, incorporating
tableware, lamps and
decorative items, all of
mottled plastic. The company
made no attempt to imitate
any traditional design
material and advertised its
products on the basis of their
cheapness and durability.

Below 'Smith Sectric' clock, phenolic and urea. Manufacturers were quick to see the advantages of plastics and this clock was both stylish and inexpensive.

Above 'Brownie' camera designed by Walter Dorwin Teague for Eastman Kodak, 1936. Teague worked for Kodak for thirty years from 1927 and this was one of his most successful products. Plastic was used since it was cheap, tough and easily moulded.

Left 'AD65' radio designed by Wells Coates for Ekco, 1933. The drum shape of Coates's cabinet expresses the machined quality of the bakelite, and the technological aspect of the design is further emphasized by the chrome gilt. This truly pioneering concept bears little resemblance to any previous radios.

Below Powder graters, 1920s, and (*opposite*) assorted powder-compacts and cigarette-cases, with a cardboard box by Coty and a glass box by Lalique. As women became more emancipated in the twenties they required more accessories, particularly for the daring new practices of smoking and using make-up.

Left Cigarette case of silver and enamel, English, 1931. Women's accessories were available at every level, from the expensive and handmade such as this to the cheapest transfer-printed nickel items.

Below Glass scent-bottles in the shape of bow ties, made by Baccarat for Guerlain of Paris. The cosmetic industry paid great attention to packaging and produced very chic designs for its elegant clientele.

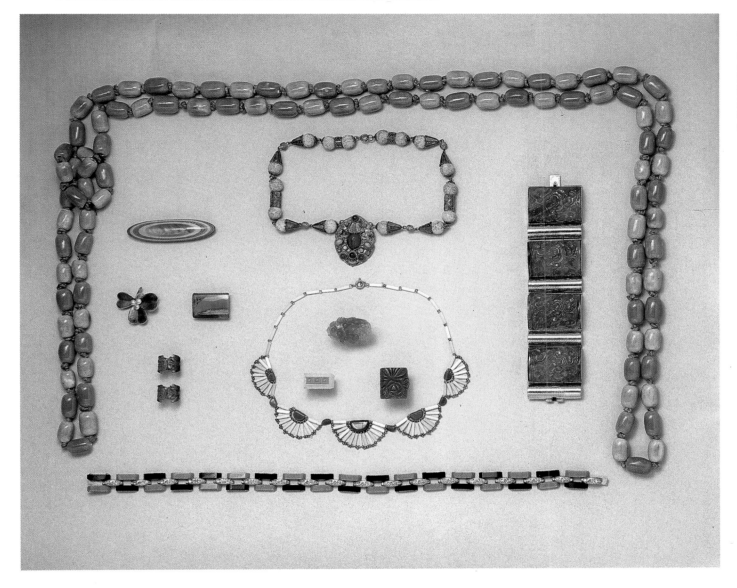

Left and opposite Costume jewellery, 1920s and 1930s. Chanel was partially responsible for making costume jewellery fashionable. Plastics lent themselves to jewellery of all kinds, and ceramics and coloured glass also enjoyed a vogue.

Mlle Nikitina
Chanel - Le Monnier
377

31

Clothes by Chanel, 1929 (*above*) and 1934 (*right*). Chanel's particular style and the apparent simplicity of her designs were highly influential at this period. They were copied for dress patterns and by home dressmakers.

Above Paper patterns, 1930s. During the Depression the paper-pattern industry flourished and magazines would often give away a pattern, illustrating the finished result on the cover. The complexity of the clothes, however, posed quite a problem for the home dressmaker.

In the period following the Second World War there was a reaction against the styles of the thirties, and in America and Italy, for example, there was a movement away from the machine aesthetic and streamlining towards a more sculptural and organic basis for design. This is perhaps most clearly seen in design for furniture, where developments in plastics and in the treatment of plywood lent themselves well to biomorphic forms. Architecture, on the other hand, tended to be a bland version of the International style with no reference at all to the stylish forms of pre-war Deco. Having said this however, it is difficult to determine exactly when Deco ended. There is plenty of evidence of Deco streamlining in the design of electrical appliances well into the fifties, and it is worth remembering that Frank Lloyd Wright's Guggenheim Museum, with its aggressively streamlined design of 1942, was not actually built until 1959. The revival of interest in the Deco period can be first discerned in the early sixties, so it seems that the style had barely passed into history before it was being re-assessed. Initially, though, it was the extravagant Deco of the twenties which attracted popular interest.

It is not difficult to understand why the twenties should have held such a particular fascination for a post-war generation searching for excitement after the years of austerity. Viewed from a distance the legendary hectic gaiety of the period and the more raffish attractions of Prohibition and organized crime acquired a powerful glamour. This was recognized by film-makers and at the end of the fifties *Some Like it Hot* and *The George Raft Story* appeared, the first films in an ultimately huge crop dealing with the twenties. Television offered *The Roaring Twenties* and *The Untouchables*, neither of which was memorable for its period accuracy, but they did give some indication of public interest.

By the middle of the sixties the renewal of interest in Deco was apparent on two levels. A serious re-evaluation of the style resulted in exhibitions like 'Les Années 25—Art Deco, Bauhaus, Stijl, Esprit Nouveau' held in Paris in 1966 and the 'Jazz Age' in 1969, which launched a new permanent collection of Deco in the Brighton Museum. The publication in 1968 of Bevis Hillier's book *Art Deco of the Twenties and Thirties* introduced a serious and informed view of the style to a wide public, and established the term 'Art Deco', which has now become universal. By the beginning of the seventies there had been several exhibitions on or relating to Deco on both sides of the Atlantic, as well as an infinite series of magazine articles ranging from the scholarly to the purely frivolous.

On another level, Deco was one of the many styles plundered in the great eclecticism of the late sixties. It was still possible then to find good Deco pieces in markets and junk shops, and although the chances of coming across a Ruhlmann screen were fairly remote, there were plenty of examples of ceramics, decorative objects, accessories, light-fittings and larger pieces of furniture which could be picked up cheaply. In England, as in America, many Deco buildings were being demolished or gutted; cinemas, for instance, were being modernized

Vegetable dish by Susie Cooper, 1950s. The shapes of this service for Crown remained unchanged from the thirties but the surface pattern was modified. Rather than being an example of revivalism this piece illustrates the durability of some Deco design.

and the decorative fixtures and fittings replaced. Much domestic Deco had been discarded in the fifties when it was simply regarded as old-fashioned and, similarly, companies which had expressed their prosperity in the twenties and thirties by having their boardrooms and offices decorated in the latest style were ready for a facelift by the sixties. PEL furniture was replaced with Scandinavian wood or moulded plastic from Italy, and chrome or bronze light-fittings with fluorescent strip.

It was not just serious collectors who were buying. At the end of the sixties Deco was used in interiors and costume as a fashionable decorative device, along with a wide variety of other near-antique and ethnic styles. In this context the name on a piece mattered less than how typical it was. Probably the best known exponent of this kind of eclecticism was Barbara Hulanicki's firm Biba. The second and third of the Biba shops in Kensington, London, were decorated in a style which lay half way between Deco and Art Nouveau and the clothes, accessories and objects marketed by the firm showed the same mixture of influences, with thirties-inspired satins hanging next to Kate Greenaway smocks, and jazz-patterned jewellery sharing counter space with Art Nouveau cutlery. When in 1973 Biba made their final move to the Derry & Toms store in Kensington High Street the Deco interior of the building was retained, dictating the overall styling of the fixtures and fittings, and the design of the Biba packaging.

Along with Art Nouveau, which was being rediscovered at the same time, Deco became a motif to be used in almost every context, often mixed with other styles. The sunburst, the ziggurat, speed stripes and lightning bolts appeared with Art Nouveau swirls in late sixties graphics, particularly in the 'underground' press, and the Beatles' animated film *Yellow Submarine* (1968) used a mixture of these styles in much of its footage.

Deco was perhaps the only style to emerge whole from the melting pot of late sixties design. The serious re-evaluation which had begun in the middle of the decade continued, and although the emphasis still remained on the acknowledged masters of the style, more obscure areas of Deco were discussed and more artists and designers were reappraised. The process has continued in the States and in Europe well into the eighties and has, in fact, lasted as long as the style itself. Meanwhile, the popular response to Deco has remained constant, original objects are still sought after, and there is an enormous quantity of reproduction Deco on the market. Some of it is simply 'in the spirit' of Deco and trades on the instantly recognizable hallmarks of the style for its impact. Deco-esque light-fittings retail in chain stores, picture frames feature stepped sides, and table-lamps made in the shape of streamlined ladies brandishing globes are a cliché now because they are so familiar. At the other end of the scale exact reproductions of named pieces have come onto the market within the last decade, ranging from copies of Chiparus's bronze and ivory figures (a trap for the unwary since some of them have copies of the signature too) to carefully made reproductions of Deco furniture. Chairs by Hoffmann, Aalto and Saarinen are all available and, recently, selected pieces of Clarice Cliff's work have been reproduced, selling for considerably less than the present price of the originals. Such reproductions indicate that the demand for Deco still exists and that it outstrips the supply of surviving original pieces.

Television and the cinema have responded to this popular interest in the style and the period which it represents. From relatively humble beginnings, an increasingly elaborate series of dramas have appeared over the last fifteen years. In the cinema *The Boyfriend*, *The Sting*, *The Great Gatsby*, *Pennies from Heaven* and *The Cotton Club* have all dealt more or less successfully with the period, while television has responded with *Tender Is the Night*, several P.G Wodehouse series and, most recently, *Mapp and Lucia*, in addition to a proliferation of advertisements with very obvious Deco styling.

In the end it is not this reproduction of the style which is the most interesting aspect of the Deco revival: it is the examination of the elements which made Deco so successful in the first place, which has in turn led to new forms in the various design disciplines. Commercial artists were perhaps the first to see the potential of the style. In America in the seventies the Pushpin Studios, run by Milton Glaser and Seymour Chwast, were applying Deco stylization to modern ends on projects as diverse as record covers, book jackets and illustrations, and advertisements. Their work cannot be seen as simple pastiche because it uses the language to create new moods, new images and new typefaces. Other designers have used elements from Deco architecture and textiles to create specific moods in advertising and packaging.

Painters, too, have responded to Deco, primarily to the two-dimensional abstraction of Deco ornament. Frank Stella at the end of the sixties produced a series of paintings called collectively the 'Protractor' series which dealt on a monumental scale with intricate patterns related to the archetypal sunburst motif. These works are unabashedly decorative, the sweet colours and curving shapes holding the attention of the viewer long before the complexities of the composition become apparent. The scale of the works, too, is extremely important and several of the pictures are over ten feet in length so the patterns are on an architectural scale. In this sense they work in much the same way as the surface detailing on twenties Deco buildings, occupying an area somewhere between graphics, architecture and sculpture. During the same period the Pop artist Roy Lichtenstein also was dealing with Deco motifs in painting and sculpture. The works are given names like *Modern Painting* or *Modern Sculpture*, but their forms are related to Deco stylization and decoration, not the fine art tradition of modernism. One of the *Modern Sculpture* pieces, for example, is clearly a decorative barrier from a movie house or theatre, complete with its rope. Although the *Modern Art* series is certainly quite tongue-in-cheek, it can also be seen as a shrewd comment on the nature of the relationship between the fine and decorative arts. Deco was a useful language for a number of Pop artists in the late sixties, as the flat colours and hard-edged shapes of Deco graphics were particularly appropriate for Pop imagery. One artist who has taken the style further is David Hockney. There is no sense in which his paintings can be seen as Deco pastiches but they do use the language and forms in a very knowing manner, particularly in the Los Angeles and Hollywood pictures where the colours and simplified forms relate to the Deco graphic tradition while the technique is painterly in a sophisticated way.

Perhaps the most surprising aspect of the Deco revival is that it should have had any effect on architecture, surprising because architecture is traditionally the most conservative of the disciplines and the most reluctant to adopt a fashion. For the two decades following the Second World War, Deco was a discredited style in architecture, regarded by disciples of the International school as being frivolous— the zeal with which many fine Deco buildings were demolished during the fifties and sixties is evidence of this rejection. By the mid-fifties the influence of the International style was dominant in architecture on both sides of the Atlantic. As early as 1966, however, the architect Robert Venturi was suggesting ideas for an alternative language. In his book *Complexity and Contradiction in Architecture* he argues the case for buildings which use a mixed range of styles and vernacular, operating on a symbolic level as well as a purely utilitarian one. Although he does not specifically mention Deco in the book, the criteria he lays down are an almost perfect description of something like the Chrysler Building. A little later Venturi and other architects, most specifically Michael Graves, were quite outspoken in their defence of Art Deco architecture, which they felt had succeeded where the International style was doomed by its very nature to fail.

Michael Graves's own work after the mid-seventies incorporated a great deal of Deco imagery. The Portland Public Services Building in Portland, Oregon, uses Deco language in its overall shape, the ordering of the windows, and in the nature and distribution of the surface decoration. His Humana Medical Corporation Building from Louisville, Kentucky, makes reference to skyscrapers with their monumental entrances and porches, while its tower ends in a modified ziggurat.

In Europe the Memphis design group from Milan have also produced architectural designs which show a very heavy Deco influence. Nathalie du Pasquier's *City* from 1983 is an assemblage of forms, including ziggurats and pyramid shapes, with detailing entirely reminiscent of twenties Deco, and Ettore Sottsass has designed skyscrapers which are intended to function as symbols of commerce and finance in the same way as the early prototypes. In becoming one of the main languages of Post-Modernist architecture, Deco has also gone some way towards saving itself, for in America at least many fine Deco buildings are now preserved by law. In the development of American Deco, architecture influenced the other design disciplines and this remains true in the Deco revival. Both Venturi and Graves have turned their hands to designing furniture and small-scale objects in a Deco manner. Memphis, too, has made constant reference to twenties and thirties shapes and colours in their wooden furniture from the end of the seventies and laminate furniture from the early eighties, but the language is not treated reverently and decorative elements are frequently taken out of context or translated—fluted surfaces in the manner of Betty Joel appear as striped laminate, inlay as screen-printed laminate. Michael Graves in his work for Memphis uses forms which come very directly from American Deco and are instantly recognizable as such: his 'Stanhope' bed from 1982 makes reference to movie house architecture and his 'Plaza' dressing-table from 1981 to the Radio City Music Hall tradition, right down to the mirror-glass columnettes which flank the central mirror.

There are many young craftspeople in Europe and America who have looked to various aspects of Deco for inspiration and the range of references seems to be widening. Initially the prime source was twenties Deco and this still remains important to those who are producing furniture, jewellery and so on. The work of Americans like Judy Kensley McKie and Jack Larimore, both furniture makers, or William Scholl and Eric Russell, both jewellers, shows a clear debt to the tradition of the unique object. Also the whole area of mass-produced Deco is now being re-examined not necessarily by people who are themselves mass-producing but by those who are looking at the forms of industrial design and streamlining. The work of Nicky Noyes uses the language of popular and mass-produced Deco, and in some ways he could be said to be dealing with the archetypal forms since some of his designs are so simplified.

Again, in the tradition of American Deco, revival designers who began as makers of exclusive and often very expensive pieces have turned their hands to design for mass production. Venturi has designed china for the Swid Powell company and Graves a tea-service for Alessi, both of which are Deco in inspiration. As yet we have no equivalent of a Russel Wright or a Norman Bel Geddes—a Deco revivalist working for industry—although there is some evidence of the influence of stream-lining in products like the Sharp radio-cassette player, which has a smoothed, curving case complete with incised lines reminiscent of speed stripes and comes in a variety of Deco-esque colours, including ivory. Visually, the radio stands opposed to the high-tech styling of mainstream radio and personal stereo products. Textile companies have mass-produced Deco-inspired fabrics and Liberty has marketed various ranges which have not been copies of original twenties or thirties designs but, like Post-Modernist architecture, have used the language. Similarly firms which design and produce wallpapers and wrapping papers have adopted Deco motifs. Nigel Quiney Designs, for example, produce a wrapping paper called 'Aztec' which is based on two designs from the exterior of Frank Lloyd Wright's Hollyhock house. The influence of thirties industrial design can also be seen in the products marketed by firms like Practical Styling in London, whose very name is reminiscent of PEL—Practical Equipment Limited.

It is perhaps inaccurate to call the influence of Deco on modern design a 'revival' at all. Revivals tend to evoke a wish to return to the past and in its initial stages the Deco revival can be seen in exactly that light—Biba for example was heavily saturated with nostalgia—but the direction of design now is too vigorous and perhaps too aggressive to fit comfortably into the rather cosy ambience of a revival. Since we are no longer dealing with history we can only speculate as to what direction the revival will ultimately take, or what long-term effects Post-Modernism will have on the urban landscape and interior. In the sense that the revival has stopped the destruction of some of its original sources, it has already had an effect and Deco has certainly entered the visual vocabulary of many people too young to have ever experienced it first hand.

Radio-cassette player by Sharp, 1984. Though this format is a relatively recent one it has been given Deco styling with a streamlined shape and bright colouring.

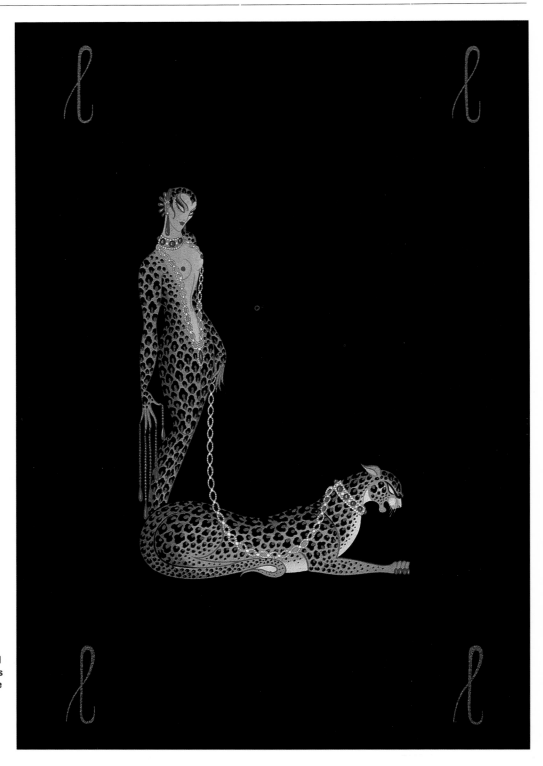

Right: L from an alphabet by Erté (Romain de Tirtoff), 1976–7. Erté's particular brand of Deco graphics remained largely unchanged for sixty years. His work was much sought after during the early stages of the Deco revival, and since he was still working he was able to supply new work in the same style.

Above **Jacket by Bentley,**
Farrell, Burnett for ***The World***
of Art Deco **by Bevis Hillier.**
Published as the catalogue of
the exhibition organized by
the Minneapolis Institute of
Arts in 1971, this book was a
landmark in the Deco revival.
The jacket is one of the finest
examples of revival graphics.

Below and opposite Interior of Biba, Derry & Toms' Building, London, 1973. In this virtually intact Deco building Biba were able to recreate an entire Deco experience which became a high point of the revival. Unfortunately commercial pressures overwhelmed the business after only a few years and the store closed.

Above: Pennies from Heaven,
1982. Since *The Boyfriend*
there have been a number of
Deco-inspired films.

Below: **The Boyfriend**, a film of Sandy Wilson's thirties pastiche by Ken Russell, 1970. In a loving parody of a Busby Berkeley film, Russell made full use of elaborate set-piece dance routines pinned to a minimal plot.

Graphics by Seymour Chwast of the Pushpin Studios, New York. In the sixties Pushpin were among the first to make intelligent use of Deco graphics. Their designs were, and continue to be, witty and inventive, whether used for posters, book jackets or three-dimensional objects.

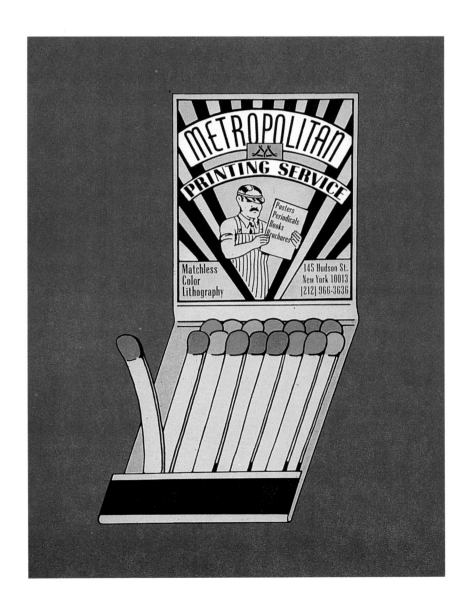

Above: Lac La Ronge by
Frank Stella, 1968. One of a
group of paintings produced
by Stella in the late sixties,
this uses flat, sweet colours
reminiscent of Deco graphics
and interior design.

Right: Modern Sculpture by
Roy Lichtenstein, around
1967. Lichtenstein derived the
forms for this series from
Deco theatre and movie-
house furniture—bannisters,
barriers, door handles and so
on. There is also a passing
reference to the high-style
Deco of designers like Eileen
Gray.

Right Public Services
Building, Portland, Oregon,
by Michael Graves, 1980–2.
In this sophisticated blend of
Deco and classicism the
stepped tower of a thirties
skyscraper has been
truncated. A Post-Modern
'column' and 'capital', flat
and highly graphic, dominate
the facade and a Deco frieze
tops the windows of the side
elevation.

Above Portico, Humana Building. This shows clear Deco references in its geometric decoration, stepped-back wall areas and 'machined' classical detailing.

Left Humana Building, Louisville, Kentucky, by Michael Graves, 1982–5. In this Post-Modern version of a thirties skyscraper the language of classicism is adapted in scale and function. With its 'head' and 'legs' it is, like the Chrysler Building, curiously anthropomorphic, and in the skyscraper tradition it has a monumental entrance at street level.

Right 'Plaza' dressing-table designed by Michael Graves for Memphis, 1981. The complex Deco imagery of this piece includes the mirror-glass columnettes which flank the mirror, the lighting globes and the very conception of a 'dressing-table'. Even the name is Deco. The design can also be seen as a miniature skyscraper with the mirror set in the stepped tower and the base forming the street-level entrance.

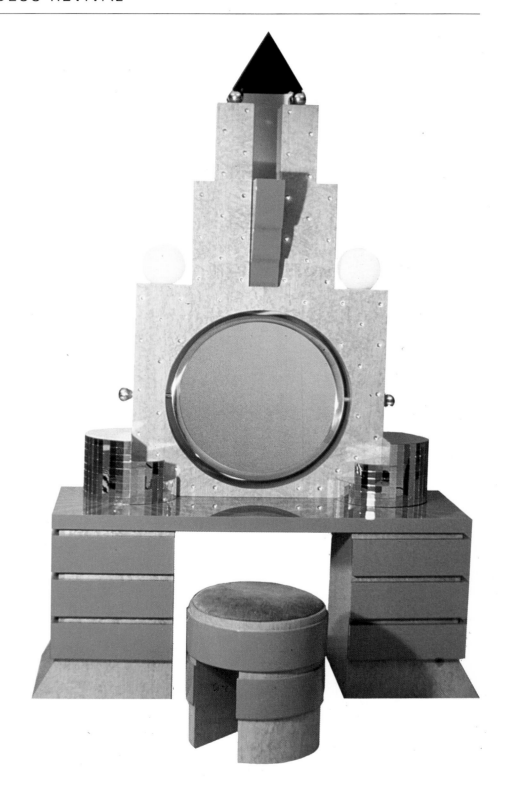

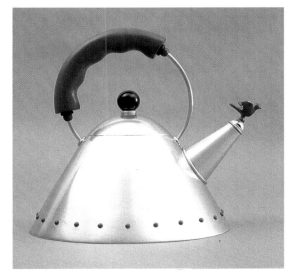

Left Tea kettle designed by Michael Graves for Alessi. With its playful references to modernism, Graves's tea kettle has something in common with Donald Deskey's designs from the thirties. The strongly stated functionalism is repudiated by the little bird which is the whistle.

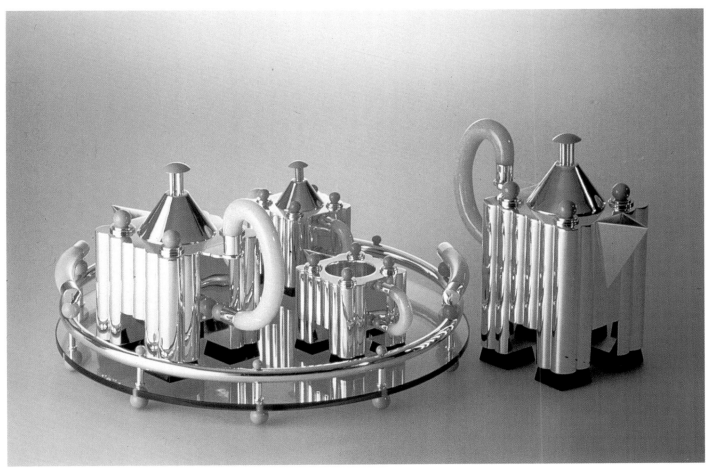

Left Tea service designed by Michael Graves for Alessi, 1983. The pieces sit like little skyscrapers on the tray, which itself is derived from the glass-and-chrome trolleys of the twenties. The influence of Deco can also be seen in the little blue knobs and the exaggerated handles.

Right 'Beverly' by Ettore Sottsass for Memphis, 1981. Such are the innumerable references to Deco in this piece that it becomes a playful visual 'history' of Deco design. The printing on the cupboard doors is reminiscent of shagreen, a favourite surface covering of Deco furniture, and the chrome bar supporting the light is an obvious reference to thirties furniture.

Below 'Ball Top' table, marble and, wood designed by Jack Larimore. Like the Deco of the twenties, Larimore's work plays with historical styles, in this case Egyptian. The mixture of organic and precious materials was also a feature of twenties design.

Above Ceramics for Memphis. The play on Deco shapes is an important element in these pieces, recalling both 'jazz'-inspired twenties ceramics and Deco graphics. The pyramid and triangular shapes have been exaggerated so the function of the objects becomes secondary to the sculptural silhouette.

Left The De Menil house, East Hampton, by Gwathmey Siegal & Associates, 1983. The house is Corbusian in inspiration and makes many references to the architecture of the thirties. The glass wall of the bathroom, for instance, is ultimately derived from Pierre Chareau's Maison de Verre of 1928 in Paris.

Above and opposite The Swid apartment, New York, by Gwathmey Siegal & Associates, 1984. Specifically designed to house a collection of Deco and Werkstätte furniture, the interior is Deco-like in its use of artificial lighting to emphasize the spatial forms, and also in such details as the lacquered portals and modified streamlining.

Right Interior, TVAM studios.
This is more overtly Deco,
with innumerable references
to ziggurats, supporting
columns (similar to those in
the Johnson Wax Building)
and fully integrated lighting.

Right **TVAM, London, by Terry Farrell, 1983. The street facade, with its long curve and emphatic speed stripes, is a play on streamlining. Other Deco references include the skeletal monumental entrance and the incorporation of modernist graphics into the architecture.**

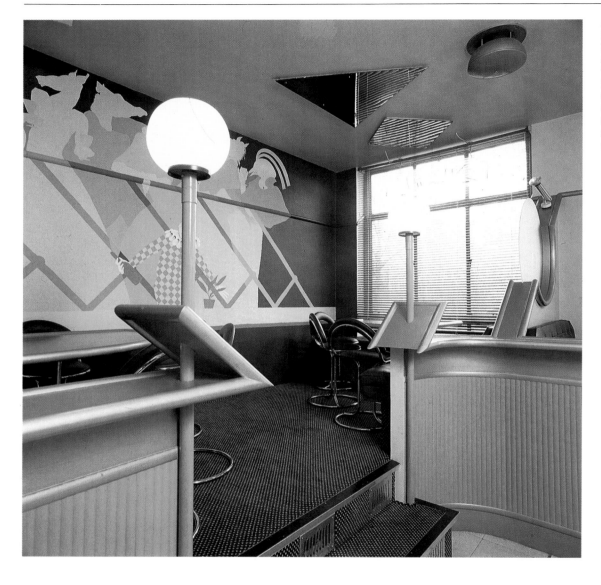

Left Jacques Bar, Tavistock Hotel, London, by Piers Gough, 1980. The twenties saw the introduction of the 'cocktail' and therefore Deco has become the natural decorative language for cocktail bars. In recent years almost every bar has adopted a version of the glass-and-chrome American Deco.

Opposite Unilever House, London, by Theo Crosby at Pentagram, 1984. Deco in its zigzag imagery, integrated lighting and eclectic historical references, this foyer is a true descendant of the great interiors of twenties skyscrapers.

Right and below Easy chair and sofa by Nicky Noyes. Using archetypal Deco forms and fabrics in a highly exaggerated manner, Noyes creates something entirely modern in feeling.

Below Chairs, designed by Robert Venturi for Knoll, 1984. Just as Deco designers used with total license historical source material for stylistic ends, so Venturi adapts the classic Chippendale chair and gives it a deliberately graphic, decorative and two-dimensional quality.

Below Triangular brooch by Patricia Dudgeon, 1986; ebony, aquamarine and platinum. Semicircular brooch by Sharon de Meza, 1986; diamonds and platinum. The abstract, geometric shapes, the machined finish and even the materials recall Deco jewellery. Platinum was very fashionable in the thirties.

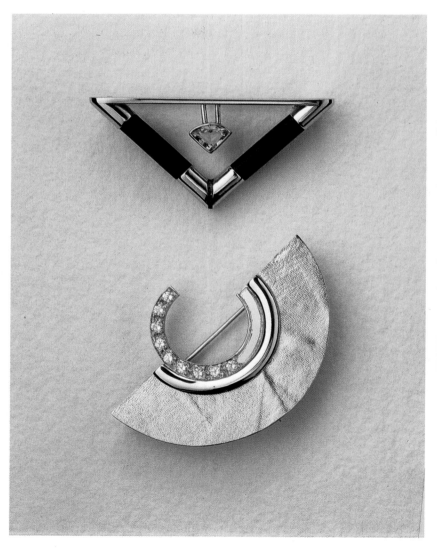

Above Pendant by Eric Russell. As in Deco jewellery, these pieces include Egyptian imagery, bold formalizations and a deliberately machined quality.

Left Glass and gold necklace by Linda McNeil, 1984. Both Linda McNeil and her husband Dan Daley, who also works in glass, would readily acknowledge their debt to Deco. She makes ample use of the sleek geometry, the shapes strengthened by her preference for primary colours.

Below Pewter earrings and bangles by Gill Clements, 1986. These designs recall one of the favourite Deco sources, that of African art. The zigzag design, along with the ziggurat, is one of the archetypal Deco patterns.

Below Wrapping papers and gift card by Nigel Quiney Designs, 1980–2. Art Deco has been a strong influence on ephemera since the sixties. These designs have been inspired by Frank Lloyd Wright, by Dufy and by what can best be described as a Deco 'mood'.

Above Illustration by Lon Goddard, around 1980. This exploits both the style and the mood of late thirties films.

Below:*KFY In The Sky*, greetings card by David Juniper for Heroes Stationery, 1979. As a style Deco lends itself to airbrush techniques, and it persists as an important element of advertising and graphic design.

Above Poster for London Transport by Ken Cox, 1979. This is a deliberate recreation of the style of London Transport posters of the thirties.

Arwas, Victor. *Art Deco*. London, 1980.

Banham, Reyner. *Theory and Design in the First Machine Age*. London, 1960.

Battersby, Martin. *The Decorative Thirties*. London, 1969.

Battersby, Martin, *The Decorative Twenties*. London, 1971.

Brownlow, Kevin. *The Parade's Gone By*. London, 1968.

Brunhammer, Yvonne. *The Art Deco Style*. London, 1983.

Buckle, Richard. *Diaghilev*. London, 1979.

Camard, Florence. *Ruhlmann: Master of Art Deco*. London, 1984.

Delhaye, Jean. *Art Deco Posters and Graphics*. London, 1977.

Department of Overseas Trade. *Reports on the Present Position and Tendencies of the Industrial Arts as Indicated at the International Exhibition of Modern Decorative and Industrial Arts, Paris, 1925*. London, 1927.

Desky, D. 'The Rise of American Architecture and Design', *The Studio*, no 5, April 1933, London.

Ferriss, Hugh. *The Metropolis of Tomorrow*. New York, 1929.

Frankl, Paul. *Form and Re-Form*. New York, 1930.

Haslam, Malcolm. *Marks and Monograms of the Modern Movement 1875–1930*. London, 1977.

Haslam, Malcolm. *The Real World of the Surrealists*. London, 1978.

Hennessey, William J. *Russel Wright: American Designer*. Cambridge, Mass., 1983.

Hillier, Bevis. *Art Deco*. New York, 1968.

Hitchcock, Henry-Russell. *Architecture: Nineteenth and Twentieth Centuries*. London, 1971.

HMSC *Art and Industry*. London, 1932.

Howell, Georgina. *In Vogue*. London, 1975.

Huddleston, Sisley. *Bohemian, Literary and Social Life in Paris*. London, 1928.

Jenkins, Alan. *The Twenties*. London, 1974.

Kjellberg, Pierre. *Art Deco: Les Maîtres du Mobilier*. Paris, 1981.

La Vine, Robert. *In a Glamorous Fashion*. London, 1981.

Lesieutre, Alain. *The Spirit and Splendour of Art Deco*. London, 1981.

Lloyd Wright, Frank. *A Testament*. New York, 1957.

Meikle, Jeffrey L. *Twentieth Century Ltd*. Philadelphia, 1979.

Naylor, Gillian. *The Bauhaus*. London, 1968.

Noble, David F. *America By Design*. New York, 1977.

Open University. *British Design*. Course unit 19 & 20, A305. Milton Keynes, 1975.

Open University. *The New Objectivity*. Course unit 11 & 12, A305. Milton Keynes, 1975.

Open University. *USA 1890–1939*. Course unit 7 & 8, A305. Milton Keynes, 1975.

Pevsner, Nikolaus. *Pioneers of Modern Design*. London, 1960.

Pevsner, Nikolaus. *The Sources of Modern Architecture and Design*. London, 1968.

Radice, Barbara. *Memphis*. New York, 1984.

Sachs, Maurice. *Au temps du Bœuf sur le Toît*. Paris, 1939.

Schindle, Norman G. 'Beauty Doctors Take a Hand in Automobile Design', *Automotive Industries*, 13 August 1927, USA.

Vergo, Peter. *Art in Vienna 1898–1918*. London, 1975.

Weber, Eva. *Art Deco in America*. New York, 1985.

White, Palmer. *Poiret*. London, 1973.

Whitney Museum of American Art. *High Styles: Twentieth-Century American Design*. Exhibition catalogue. New York, 1985.

Wolfe, Elsie de. *After All*. London, 1935.